Staying Rich

Staying Rich

Inside the Financial Habits, Social Codes, and Hidden Strategies That Keep the Wealthy Wealthy

Julian C. Vale

Mindful Pages

Published in 2025

ISBN: 9789371770064 (PB)
ISBN: 9789371770422 (eBook)

Published by

Mindful Pages
Imprint of Alpha Editions LLC
312 W. 2nd St #1834
Casper, WY 82601, USA

This book was developed using advanced writing tools to support the drafting and ideation process. All content has been thoughtfully curated, refined, and reviewed to ensure quality and relevance.

Content

Introduction
Why Staying Rich Is a Different Skillset Than Getting Rich

There is an unseen architecture underpinning enduring wealth—one seldom discussed in popular finance books, podcasts, or interviews. It is not built on sheer ambition, flash innovation, or headline-grabbing returns. Rather, it relies on insulation, discretion, discipline, and a quiet structural advantage. Contrary to common perception, wealth is not merely created; it is actively defended. And the instincts, frameworks, and behaviours required for defence are often distinct—sometimes entirely opposed—to those that generated the fortune in the first place.

Our culture obsesses over ascent: the scrappy founder, the meteoric startup, the rags-to-riches narrative. We are told endlessly about the psychology and mechanics of getting rich—tales of grit, hustle, and exponential growth fill shelves and screens. But what happens after the applause fades, after volatility begins its patient work? This book turns its focus to that quieter, less glamorous frontier: the art of staying rich.

A striking pattern emerges on closer inspection: many new fortunes are fragile. They crumble not solely through recklessness, but through unexamined assumptions. Those who accumulate wealth often assume that the strategies which lifted them will sustain them. Yet the logic of accumulation and the logic of endurance differ fundamentally, sometimes even clash. Speed gives way to patience. Visibility becomes vulnerability. Leverage is replaced by liquidity. Where entrepreneurs chase opportunity, the enduring wealthy design resilience.

This disconnect underpins much conventional financial advice, which assumes linearity: budget more, save more, invest sooner, work harder. Such guidance speaks to the psychology of scarcity, not preservation. It presumes the reader is still building wealth, not defending it. Little counsel addresses the subtler dilemmas of abundance: how to protect assets without stagnation, how to limit exposure without forfeiting growth, how to teach heirs judgment, not just inheritance.

Staying rich demands a different lens. It is about architecture, not aspiration. It is about creating durable legal, psychological, relational, and informational systems that safeguard capital quietly over time. True wealth is not defined by what one can gain, but by what one can protect from erosion.

The principle is simple: endurance follows different rules than accumulation. It is governed not by aggressive growth but by exposure control. Those who preserve wealth think in terms of insulation rather than ambition. Their central question is rarely "How do I make more?" but "What am I blind to?" They cultivate an anticipatory mindset, recognising that most losses emerge from unplanned extremes rather than everyday fluctuations.

Consider economic shocks—the 2008 financial crisis or the liquidity crunch during COVID. Wealth did not merely transfer hands; it evaporated for some while compounding for others. The decisive factor was not prior returns but how exposure had been structured. Some were forced to sell; others had the luxury to wait. Some acted merely to survive; others acted to gain. That quiet gulf between positions is the terrain this book seeks to illuminate.

Contrary to popular belief, the wealthy are rarely reckless risk-takers. They are risk designers. They compartmentalise exposure, protect downside, and maintain options for volatility to become opportunity. This is not instinct alone; it is methodical. Liquidity, structures, and the orchestration of systems create defensive intelligence, enabling calculated action—or deliberate inaction.

We will examine how wealthy families embed strategic conservatism across their lives: from raising children to structuring ownership, from cultivating networks to treating silence as an asset.

Terms like "dry powder," "strategic retreat," "quiet move," and "off-market flow" signify more than jargon—they encode a worldview attentive to time, volatility, and discretion.

This book does not idolise wealth or romanticise the rich. Its aim is empirical: to reveal mechanisms that preserve capital over decades, asking which behaviours can be replicated, which cannot, and what hidden costs and rewards lie behind visible fortune and discretion.

Each chapter explores a dimension of wealth endurance. We begin by critiquing conventional financial advice, showing how it reflects the needs of accumulation, not preservation. We then delve into intergenerational intelligence, liquidity as resilience, the psychology of restraint, strategic boredom, the value of unglamorous assets, and the outsized influence of social capital. We analyse risk across jurisdictions, asset classes, legal structures, and emotional bandwidth.

Underlying it all is a single insight: enduring wealth privileges optionality. Control, timing, and non-reactivity outweigh glamour or speed. The capacity to abstain from action is itself a form of power.

This book does not promise shortcuts or guarantees. It offers structures, strategies, and perspectives to sharpen understanding of what money can—and cannot—achieve. Whether you are wealthy, approaching wealth, or merely seeking insight, the goal is clarity over dazzlement.

In a world seduced by growth, spectacle, and noise, there is wisdom in doing less, speaking less, and exposing less without ceding ground. Quiet moves, disciplined retreats, and engineered margins are not signs of inertia—they are the instruments of enduring wealth. Those who maintain it do not simply get richer; they think differently. And now, so can you.

Chapter 1
The Illusion of Sameness

Most financial guidance circulating today is not aimed at those who already possess wealth, nor at those within striking distance of it. It is overwhelmingly tailored to people striving to escape precarity, couched in the language of discipline, sacrifice, and incrementalism. Budgets, side hustles, compound interest as salvation, caffeine habits as moral failing—these are the mantras of ascent. And while such counsel serves its purpose for those starting their climb, it becomes actively misleading when applied to individuals whose priorities are closer to capital preservation than accumulation.

The allure is easy to succumb to: the notion that money is universal, that financial wisdom is one-size-fits-all. But money, like language, behaves differently depending on the speaker and the audience. A single portfolio strategy carries different implications depending on your starting point. A market correction can spell catastrophe for some and opportunity for others. Advice presented as neutral is often laden with class assumptions, subtle enough to go unnoticed—until they do not.

Take the oft-repeated maxim: "Invest early, hold long, ride volatility." Sound counsel for someone with a long horizon and ample cushions. But for those whose liquidity is thin or timelines short, it can be perilous. The instruction to "stay the course" implicitly assumes resilience—psychological and practical—and access to capital when markets turn sour.

Risk, too, is framed differently across economic strata. For the average household, it manifests as income loss, savings depletion, or lifestyle erosion—a medical emergency, redundancy, or housing crisis. Wealth, in contrast, frames risk as exposure: a variable to be modelled, transferred, insured, or externalised. It is not merely endured; it is designed, mitigated, and occasionally exploited. Herein lies a profound asymmetry.

High-net-worth individuals seldom "take risks" as popularly imagined. Bold moves—large investments, complex ventures, contrarian bets—are frequently buffered by quiet safeguards: trusts, credit lines, layered ownership structures, informal backstops. Capital is rarely deployed en masse; exposure is ringfenced. Middle-class actors, by contrast, often operate all-in, knowingly or not.

This exposes one of the more insidious fallacies in financial culture: the supposed polarity between "playing it safe" and "taking risks." For the wealthy, safety and growth coexist in a carefully orchestrated hierarchy. Preservation dominates expansion. Maintaining solvency under stress precedes chasing yield. The paradox is that disciplined management of downside often enables asymmetric upside, especially when others are compelled to retreat.

The wealthy operate under a doctrine of strategic restraint. They understand that saying no—holding back, declining exposure, resisting attention—is frequently the most potent move. This discipline rarely registers on conventional metrics; it is invisible, even boring. But this invisibility is deliberate, not incidental.

Quiet moves define the landscape of enduring wealth. Discreet exits from volatile sectors, allocations into less-visible yet durable instruments, early access to off-market deals—these are not mistakes of inaction, but carefully timed strategic patience. Waiting is intentional; it is accompanied by dry powder and optionality.

Privilege underpins these moves. Access—to information, decision-makers, legal infrastructure—enables risk to be structured rather than merely absorbed. The middle class often reacts to external conditions; the wealthy quietly shape them. While many scramble during downturns, the strategically positioned advance with control, having anticipated the dislocations others endure.

Wealth creates its own gravitational field. Crises magnify the effect. While the loudest players are punished by volatility, the quiet step forward, insulated and poised. This is not luck; it is a mental model prioritising endurance over enthusiasm.

Wealthy families frequently organise around avoiding irreversible outcomes. Success is measured not by winning big, but by avoiding catastrophic loss. Layers of legal protections, asset segregation, diversified income, multiple passports, geographic dispersion—these are structural, not flashy, yet they prevent a single shock from destabilising the system.

This defensive intelligence seldom attracts attention. It is not spectacular, nor does it inspire seminars or headlines. Yet it sustains capital across generations, revealing a critical truth: the objective is not merely to grow wealth, but to insulate it.

For those accustomed to conventional financial frameworks, this perspective may feel like an entirely different operating system—and that is precisely the point. Treating all advice as universally applicable is not merely mistaken; it is dangerous. It fosters overexposure, misalignment, and false confidence, prompting mimicry of behaviours without grasping their structural underpinnings.

This chapter dismantles the illusion of universality. It explains why conventional guidance must be reinterpreted through the lens of structural power. It examines how the wealthy redefine risk, why growth is secondary, and how access to informal networks alters what is feasible in moments of stress. It begins to show readers, regardless of current capital, how to shift from a mindset of hustle and hope to one of clarity and control.

Staying rich is not a matter of intelligence alone. It is a matter of constructing and operating within a different system. And often, the difference is invisible—until it is too late.

Why Most Financial Advice Is Not Meant for You

Walk into any bookshop, scan the personal finance section, and you'll see an overwhelming number of titles promising freedom, mastery, or millionaire status through some combination of budgeting, index funds, discipline, and side hustles. The packaging is modern, the language is motivational, and the case studies feel attainable. But scratch the surface and a subtle pattern emerges—

one that reveals the quiet, structural exclusion at the heart of mainstream financial advice. It is crafted, almost without exception, for people who are *trying to become wealthy*, not for those who already are, or are close to it. And more importantly, it is calibrated for a particular economic class—those with limited capital, high income dependence, and minimal structural leverage. For them, it may offer some measure of guidance. For anyone else, it is often irrelevant—or worse, actively misleading.

The most pervasive financial advice today assumes sameness. It universalises tactics that were designed under constraints specific to a particular demographic: typically, a salaried professional with limited liquidity, little or no exposure to private capital markets, and a dependence on earned income as the primary source of wealth generation. The advice is built on a kind of narrative scaffolding that places responsibility for financial success squarely on individual behaviour: *spend less*, *invest consistently*, *stay the course*, *avoid lifestyle creep.* But in doing so, it collapses class difference into a one-size-fits-all blueprint. It ignores the fact that financial options, and the consequences of financial decisions, are contextually determined. Time horizon, margin of error, risk appetite, and access to corrective resources all shift dramatically depending on one's starting point.

A budget may feel empowering to someone living month-to-month. But for a person with meaningful assets and complex obligations—such as ownership stakes, trusts, or variable cash flow across asset classes—a simple budget becomes not only insufficient but dangerously reductive. It is not just about how much is spent, but where capital is deployed, how it is protected, how it is structured for liquidity, and whether exposure is layered across correlated risks. These are not questions a traditional personal finance manual is equipped to address.

Likewise, the popular advice to *maximise income through side hustles* or *monetise your passions* can make sense when your only asset is your time. But for those with real capital—financial, relational, or reputational—time is not the scarcest resource. Optionality is. The wealthy do not typically seek to maximise every income stream available to them; they seek to optimise *exposure to downside.* They understand that overextension is more dangerous than underperformance, and that excessive hustle often reveals a lack of structural power. To someone steeped in wealth preservation thinking, the hustle ethic looks not ambitious but vulnerable.

This divergence becomes particularly visible during periods of economic stress. Mainstream financial advice tends to rely on linear stability: the idea that income can be assumed, markets will correct, and long-term compounding is inevitable if one stays the course. But this view collapses under pressure. During the 2008 financial crisis, for instance, many middle-class investors who followed standard asset allocation models saw decades of savings erode, precisely because they were overexposed to public markets without liquidity buffers. Meanwhile, wealthy individuals who appeared to be "doing nothing" were in fact executing highly strategic non-moves—redeploying dry powder, buying distressed assets off-market, or exiting positions long before the crisis was publicly acknowledged.

This is where the fundamental class asymmetry reveals itself: the wealthy have *structural resilience*, not just behavioural discipline. They don't just budget—they buffer. They don't just save—they silo risk. And most critically, they do not rely on hope, time, or motivational slogans to protect them from downside events. They use tools that are often invisible to the average reader: layered entities, offshore accounts, bespoke insurance instruments, pre-IPO deal flow, staggered tax structures, and high-cost but high-calibre advisory networks. These are not accessible to most. And yet, their absence is rarely acknowledged in mass-market financial literature, which continues to sell the idea that wealth is primarily a function of mindset and frugality.

There is also a psychological sleight of hand embedded in popular financial advice: it reframes class constraints as personal failings. If you aren't wealthy, it must be because you didn't budget well enough. If you aren't free, you didn't hustle hard enough. This reframing creates a powerful form of internalised economic pressure. It keeps people striving within systems that are structurally limited, mistaking behavioural solutions for systemic ones. This is not to say discipline is irrelevant. But when every piece of advice boils down to *personal responsibility*, it obscures the real levers of financial endurance: access, timing, ownership, and insulation from ruin.

Ownership, in particular, is a topic that mainstream advice tends to handle superficially. Buy a house. Own your car. Invest in ETFs. But these forms of ownership often come with high exposure—debt, maintenance, low liquidity. For the wealthy, ownership is often indirect, insulated, and optional. They control assets without exposing themselves fully to their liabilities. They own through entities. They separate operating risk from asset value. They use structures like holding companies, silent partnerships, and multi-layered trusts to retain upside while limiting personal downside. This is not advanced budgeting—it is advanced architecture. And it changes everything.

The same goes for timing. A great deal of standard financial advice leans on dollar-cost averaging: invest consistently, regardless of market conditions. This strategy works well for passive investors with long time horizons and little access to tactical opportunities. But it ignores the immense advantage conferred by timing—not in the speculative sense of market timing, but in the sense of strategic patience. Wealthy individuals are often less invested in constant exposure and more interested in having liquidity *at the right moment.* They value the ability to *pause*, *withhold*, or *strike when others cannot.* Their strategy is not to be fully invested all the time—it is to be *optionally* invested *at the best possible time.*

What most financial advice misses is that the truly wealthy do not make decisions from within the market—they often position themselves around it. They shape the conditions of their exposure. They are buyers when others are forced sellers, and sellers when others are euphoric. They operate on a time axis that is not bound to income cycles or annual returns. Their liquidity is not just a buffer—it is a weapon.

Perhaps most dangerously, conventional advice is silent on *fragility.* It teaches how to grow a portfolio, but not how to protect a position. It assumes that growth is always good, and more is always better. But fragility—the inability to survive negative volatility—is what actually determines endurance. Many who "invest smartly" in bull markets discover too late that they have no exit options when conditions reverse. Their assets are illiquid, their cash flow is tight, their tax obligations are triggered at the wrong moment. And they find themselves locked into a system that punishes their previous success. This is the cost of following generic advice without understanding the structural assumptions beneath it.

All of this raises a difficult but necessary question: who is financial advice *really* for? And who is it designed *by*? Most personal finance literature is not written by wealth managers, risk engineers, or capital architects. It is written by writers. Many of them well-intentioned, some of them personally successful, but few with deep experience in high-net-worth asset structuring. The result is a genre that reflects the psychology of the aspirational middle class, not the actual behaviours of the enduring wealthy.

To be clear, there is nothing inherently wrong with budgeting, saving, or investing early. But these are tools—limited tools—that must be placed within a broader context of structure, insulation, and adaptability. When presented as universal principles, they become dogma. And dogma has a way of blinding people to options that sit just outside their current worldview.

The most useful financial advice is not motivational—it is structural. It shows you how wealth is actually maintained under duress, how risk is repositioned, how control is retained even in retreat. It recognises that personal discipline is necessary but not sufficient, and that systems—not slogans—are what ultimately determine who weathers the storm and who is forced to sell in the rain.

If you are building wealth, approaching wealth, or already managing it, you deserve more than the recycled catechism of "save more, spend less." You need to understand the architecture behind wealth that lasts—not the facade of wealth that fluctuates with sentiment. And that begins by rejecting the illusion of sameness. What works for the financially fragile may not serve those seeking insulation. What builds a foundation may not preserve it. And what sounds reasonable from the outside may look reckless from within.

Financial advice must be rethought—not just for clarity, but for class specificity. Not to shame or exclude, but to illuminate the real distinctions that shape outcomes. Because while money may be counted in the same denominations, it does not behave the same way across all hands. And if you mistake one system for another, you may spend your life mastering rules that were never meant for the game you're actually playing.

How the Rich Define Risk Differently

Risk is not a universal experience. It is neither symmetrical nor democratically distributed. Despite how it is often portrayed in textbooks or investment guides—as a calculable exposure to loss measured in standard deviation or volatility—it is, in lived reality, profoundly contextual. Two individuals may hold the same financial asset, yet their exposure to risk can be worlds apart. One may be risking surplus, the other solvency. One has optionality, the other has obligations. This is not a trivial distinction; it is the fault line that separates how the rich think about risk from how everyone else is conditioned to experience it.

To most, risk is something external—something imposed upon them by market forces, job stability, housing prices, or the caprices of inflation. It is managed reactively, with tools designed to survive volatility rather than reshape it. The language of everyday financial culture reflects this defensive posture: "emergency fund," "safe assets," "hedge against inflation," "job security." These phrases betray a worldview in which risk is a threat to be endured. But the wealthy, especially those who have endured across generations, internalise a very different relationship to risk. For them, risk is a *design variable*—not simply something to avoid, but something to structure, price, isolate, transfer, or even monetise. They do not merely absorb volatility; they *manage their position* within it.

A useful way to begin understanding this contrast is through the lens of *fragility*. For most households, fragility is embedded in their basic economic structure. Income is linear, dependent on time, and often tied to a single employer or business. Assets are concentrated in primary residences and pension accounts, with limited liquidity. One serious illness, job loss, or market correction can compromise an entire household. In this environment, risk must be minimised at all costs—there is little room for error. Consequently, risk is seen as the possibility of catastrophe, not opportunity. This perception drives an obsession with predictability, even when the long-term returns of safer options are inferior.

By contrast, the enduring wealthy construct systems that assume volatility, but refuse to be *exposed* to it unnecessarily. Their first question is rarely, "How much can I make?" but "How much am I actually risking here, and from what silo?" When they take financial risk, it is almost never existential. Instead, it is isolated—through entity structures, collateral arrangements, layered ownership, or partner syndicates. They do not stake the house; they stake the sleeve. What appears to be bold risk-taking from the outside—venture capital deployments, alternative asset investments, speculative real estate bets—is often conducted from vehicles that wall off personal balance sheets from potential blowback. This is not just smart planning—it is *philosophical insulation.*

Consider how a wealthy investor might approach private equity. She may allocate capital through a family office structure with multiple trusts and LLCs, ensuring that any failure is compartmentalised. The loss, if it comes, is painful but survivable. The same investment, made by someone of modest means, could involve putting personal savings, retirement capital, or even borrowed funds into a high-risk vehicle with no institutional backstop. The same external risk—say, the underperformance of a company—carries vastly different implications. One investor loses optionality; the other faces a material downgrade in life prospects. This is the *asymmetry of exposure*, and it is central to how the rich define and shape their risk profile.

What's notable is that this thinking is not confined to financial instruments. It extends to career decisions, legal liability, geographic residence, and even reputation management. A senior executive may have personal indemnity coverage, reputational insurance through PR firms, and pre-negotiated severance clauses that guarantee a soft landing. A freelancer or small business owner, facing the same industry disruption, may have none of these. Their exposure is personal, unbuffered. One absorbs volatility with a mattress; the other with skin.

This contrast also plays out in how the rich understand *correlation.* Most people think of diversification as simply holding different asset classes—stocks, bonds, maybe some property. But correlation is a deeper concept. It asks, "How do my assets, income sources, and obligations behave in relation to each other when stress hits the system?" Wealthy individuals often work with advisors who model scenarios not based on average conditions, but on *tail events*—the rare, extreme moments when markets move violently, liquidity evaporates, and the normal rules break down. In these moments, traditional diversification often fails. But if you've siloed assets legally, if you've diversified income across jurisdictions, or if you've structured ownership to separate control from liability, your risk posture is fundamentally different. You are no longer betting on the model—you are hedged against its failure.

Another overlooked element is *time*. For most people, time is a constraint. Risk is something to be survived until conditions improve. But for the wealthy, time can be an asset—because it affords *optionality*. They are rarely forced to sell. They can wait for valuations to normalise, markets to recover, or distressed assets to become attractive. This is why liquidity is so prized: not for consumption, but for control. Liquidity allows you to define *when* you take risk. It lets you say no when others are panicking, and yes when assets are discounted. It transforms volatility from a threat into an opportunity. The middle class tends to see liquidity as idle or wasteful. The wealthy see it as leverage in disguise.

The rich are also more likely to see risk as *non-financial*. They understand that legal exposure, reputational damage, and relational entanglements can be just as destructive as bad investments. This is why they insure art collections and intellectual property, why they seek media silence during crises, why they negotiate confidentiality clauses in every serious transaction. These are not luxuries. They are expressions of a broader risk philosophy—one that recognises that value can be destroyed in ways that have nothing to do with the stock market.

Critically, this approach to risk is not about cowardice or excessive conservatism. It is about *managing for endurance*. The rich who stay rich do not fear volatility—they fear *permanence of loss*. Temporary drawdowns, if buffered properly, are survivable. But systemic, compounding exposure—unseen, uncontained—can collapse even large fortunes. This is why their default posture is to overprotect the downside. They are not optimising for the best-case scenario. They are optimising for the worst-case being non-lethal.

None of this is to suggest that all wealthy individuals are prudent or wise. Many take reckless risks and suffer accordingly. But those who remain wealthy across cycles and generations tend to exhibit a shared pattern: they treat risk as a design challenge, not a necessary evil. They think in silos, buffers, options, and structure. They understand that the true cost of risk is not its probability but its *impact*. And they ensure that no single decision, no matter how attractive, can threaten the entire structure they've built.

The implications of this thinking extend far beyond investment strategy. It changes how you assess opportunity. If you have a fragile base—no liquidity, no margin of error, no insulation—then even a promising opportunity can be dangerous. You are effectively betting on your resilience without having engineered it. But if your downside is protected, you can engage in what Nassim Taleb calls *positive optionality*—exposing yourself to upside while containing the downside. This is where enduring wealth comes from—not just taking more risk, but *taking asymmetrical risk*.

And this, ultimately, is the divergence between how the rich define risk and how others are taught to. It is not about appetite. It is about architecture. It is not about willingness to lose—it is about capacity to absorb and recover. Risk, to them, is not a gamble. It is a variable that must be shaped—using time, structure, liquidity, and legal design—to serve their strategy rather than threaten it.

Understanding this does not require millions in capital. It requires a shift in lens. Stop asking whether an opportunity is "risky" in general. Ask: *risky to whom? From what base? With what buffer?* Because until you define your exposure, you haven't defined your risk. And until you structure your downside, you are not playing the same game.

Safety vs. Growth: The Hidden Hierarchy

The phrase "playing it safe" is typically offered as a rebuke—as if safety were the refuge of the unambitious, the uninspired, or the uninitiated. In contrast, "taking risks" is lionised as the posture of visionaries, entrepreneurs, and bold thinkers. This binary has become so culturally entrenched that to choose caution in the context of wealth is often interpreted as fear or stagnation. But among families that have preserved significant wealth across generations, the exact opposite holds true. Their financial decisions do not hinge on an appetite for maximum growth, but on a structural bias toward *non-loss*. And within that orientation lies a different kind of sophistication—one that is neither timid nor aggressive, but strategically conservative in the highest sense.

To understand this, one must abandon the language of conventional personal finance, which tends to frame safety and growth as mutually exclusive ends of a behavioural spectrum. Safe equals low returns. Risk equals reward. Choose one, live with the trade-off. Yet in the architecture of enduring wealth, this framework is far too crude. Safety and growth are not ends of a spectrum—they exist within a hierarchy. And in that hierarchy, *safety comes first not because it avoids risk, but because it creates the conditions under which risk can be taken on better terms.*

The Rockefeller family offers a compelling historical example. Contrary to popular imagination, their family office did not grow through aggressive, high-yield speculation. Its longevity was anchored in legal insulation, diversified revenue streams, and tight governance protocols that protected capital against erosion, litigation, and family discord. While growth was certainly a goal, it was not the *primary constraint.* What mattered more was that the base—capital, control, cohesion—remained intact. In this respect, the family office was not a growth engine as much as a protective vessel. Its genius was less in picking winners and more in designing structures where losses, even if they occurred, could not destabilise the whole.

This inversion of priorities is deeply countercultural. The middle-class ethos—especially in its aspirational, upwardly mobile form—

tends to chase growth as a proxy for success. Safety is often treated as a luxury or a stagnation strategy. But for wealthy families with a long-term view, safety is the *precondition* for meaningful growth. Without safety, there is no strategic patience, no resilience in downturns, no ability to pass through generational transitions without liquidation. What appears conservative in the short term often proves bold in the long arc.

This is not about hoarding cash or sitting on the sidelines. Nor is it a rejection of innovation, entrepreneurship, or dynamic capital deployment. Rather, it's a reorientation: wealth is not maximised by chasing the most growth, but by designing for the *least permanent loss*. The key distinction is permanence. Temporary drawdowns are survivable. Structural impairments are not. Families who understand this behave accordingly: they seek to absorb volatility without allowing it to degrade the underlying engine of endurance.

Take the Pritzker family, whose fortune was once tied up in the Hyatt hotel empire and a constellation of other ventures. Internal disagreements and structural vulnerabilities in the family's trust arrangements eventually led to an unwinding of assets and a reallocation of wealth across various members. What followed was a reconstitution of the family's investment strategy—less about joint empire-building, more about diversified holdings with individual autonomy. Today, many of the Pritzkers continue to grow their wealth, but with an architecture that prizes *resilience over centralisation*. Again, safety comes first—not as a retreat, but as a platform.

Part of what obscures this philosophy from the public is that its moves are often invisible. Quiet exits, unleveraged ownership, minority stakes, tax-efficient vehicles, and dry powder holdings do not announce themselves. They rarely make headlines or become case studies in business schools. But their impact is profound. These strategies allow families to *be present during market opportunities without being desperate for them.* They enable growth not by chasing every trend, but by choosing their exposures with extraordinary selectivity.

To someone raised on the gospel of compound returns and early aggressive investing, this may sound counterintuitive. Isn't maximising growth in the early decades the key to wealth? The answer, as with most durable truths, is nuanced. If one has no capital, growth must of course be pursued. But once meaningful capital is in hand—whether through inheritance, liquidity events, or sustained earnings—the logic changes. The objective shifts from *accumulation* to *continuity*. And continuity is less about how fast you grow, more about how rarely you bleed.

This reorientation is particularly critical in light of *sequence risk*—the risk that negative returns early in a capital deployment period will impair the compounding effect for years, if not permanently. Wealthy investors mitigate this by staggering investments, creating liquidity buffers, and diversifying across time horizons. In doing so, they avoid the common trap of being "all-in" at the wrong moment. The point is not to predict the future, but to design systems that *do not require precision*. This is how safety becomes a form of sophistication: it eliminates the need to be right all the time.

The hierarchy of safety over growth is also reflected in how the wealthy teach their children about money. Many family offices focus not on financial performance, but on financial *literacy of exposure*. Heirs are taught to evaluate downside risk, to ask who bears liability, to understand how reputational events can affect asset classes, and to think about financial decisions in generational rather than annual terms. The question isn't "how much will it yield," but "what happens if it fails?" This shifts the posture from return-seeking to *resilience-seeking*.

Critically, this does not produce paralysis. Families who master this hierarchy do not avoid risk—they *curate* it. They take bets, fund ventures, engage in market cycles. But they do so from a place of *controlled exposure*. This allows them to enter environments others fear, because they know their downside is hedged or externalised. It is this posture—*bold, but buffered*—that underlies much of what is misread by outsiders as luck or elite access.

In this sense, "safety" is a misnomer. What wealthy families are really doing is *designing for optionality*. They create conditions where they are not *forced* to act under pressure. This capacity to pause, to assess, to wait—is a kind of power that the traditional safety/growth binary entirely misses. In the open market, opportunities are not always about who moves fastest, but about who is still standing when the crowd has panicked and fled. Those with safety baked into their systems are not retreating from opportunity—they are reserving their right to engage on better terms.

In periods of high volatility—whether financial, political, or societal—this hierarchy proves its worth. During the early days of the COVID-19 crisis, many firms scrambled for liquidity, made reactionary decisions, or had to sell assets at depressed valuations. In contrast, some ultra-wealthy family offices held positions, increased exposure selectively, or pivoted into distressed assets. Why? Because safety had already been prioritised. Their liquidity was preserved. Their operating costs were low relative to their capital base. Their strategic retreats, if needed, had been pre-mapped. What looked like passivity was, in fact, preemptive intelligence.

The great irony is that this kind of "playing it safe" often leads to *better long-term growth.* Not because the returns are higher on paper, but because they are *less interrupted.* There are fewer forced liquidations. Fewer moments of distress. Fewer restructurings. Wealth, like any system under pressure, compounds better when it doesn't fracture. And fracture rarely comes from lack of ambition—it comes from *overexposure to unknowns.*

The false binary between safety and growth collapses under scrutiny. In practice, safety is not the opposite of growth. It is its *prerequisite.* It is what allows for intelligent risk-taking, patient capital deployment, and reputational durability. Families who understand this hierarchy do not behave timidly—they behave strategically. They avoid fragility so they can court opportunity. They preserve optionality so they can survive chaos. And they remain rich not by chasing returns, but by refusing to stake what cannot be rebuilt.

This is not advice for the fearful. It is insight for the serious. Because if you plan to endure, the question is not how fast you can grow—but how little you can afford to lose.

What We Don't See: The Privilege of Quiet Moves

The most powerful financial moves are rarely visible. They are not livestreamed, sensationalised, or discussed on public panels. They are executed quietly—sometimes invisibly—through trusted intermediaries, discreet negotiations, and tightly held networks. In a world where wealth is often associated with flamboyance and public status signalling, the most enduring capital strategies are not about exposure—they are about *positioning without scrutiny*. The privilege of quiet moves is not merely a stylistic preference. It is a structural advantage, one that allows the wealthy to protect downside, seize opportunities early, and avoid reputational or financial damage when conditions turn. For those without access to this architecture, it is not just the capital that is missing—it is the *calm vantage point from which capital can be moved with precision.*

This asymmetry is often misunderstood. Many assume that the rich take bigger risks or operate with more aggressive mandates. But those who have kept wealth intact over decades tend to do the opposite. They move more slowly, exit earlier, and signal less. Their power lies not in their public influence but in their capacity to act *before* the public is aware—*or not act at all* until conditions are entirely in their favour. And they can afford this posture because they operate within environments where information, timing, and liquidity are not just assets, but *privileges* curated by closed networks.

One of the most misunderstood features of elite finance is the timing advantage. This is not just about speed—it's about *pre-market access.* Many of the wealthiest individuals do not invest in the public iteration of an opportunity—they invest in its embryonic form. A fund is seeded long before it accepts outside capital. A real estate development is structured off-market and syndication begins only after key positions are already filled. A company shows signs of impending distress, and quiet backchannel discussions begin for a debt acquisition or prepackaged restructuring. By the time the broader market sees the move, the value has largely been extracted—or the risk has already been transferred.

This is not a conspiracy. It is the consequence of *relational capital.* A family office that has quietly backed three successive ventures for a particular general partner is likely to be offered the next opportunity well before others. A high-net-worth individual with access to elite legal counsel may receive discreet warnings about pending legislative shifts. A hedge fund insider might offer an early exit window to a trusted counterpart before major portfolio rebalancing is publicly disclosed. These are not formal perks. They are *invisible reciprocities*, sustained by discretion, reputation, and the unspoken expectation of future value flow.

A particularly telling example came during the early months of the 2008 financial crisis. As the subprime mortgage contagion began to spread, a handful of wealthy families—primarily through their private banks and advisory firms—were quietly advised to de-risk exposure to mortgage-backed securities and levered financial institutions. Some were offered preferred redemptions from hedge funds. Others were provided exclusive access to customised credit facilities that preserved liquidity when public markets froze. These were not coincidences. They were the product of *embedded presence*—relationships cultivated over years, built not on transaction volume but on *insider legitimacy*. While the general public was being reassured by headlines and pundits, those inside these networks had already begun moving to safety.

But it's not just about crisis exits. The privilege of quiet moves also includes *strategic entries*—investments made before value becomes visible, and therefore before pricing reflects potential. Consider how many of the ultra-wealthy enter real estate markets not through listings, but through relationships with developers, city officials, or long-standing landowners. Properties are repositioned before being purchased. Zoning decisions are anticipated. Redevelopment plans are quietly aligned. By the time an opportunity is made public, the alpha has largely been absorbed.

The same logic applies to private equity. Many family offices gain access to operating businesses not through auctions, but through informal conversations at investment retreats, charity boards, or industry roundtables. They partner quietly, structure governance discreetly, and build value with minimal outside scrutiny. When it's time to exit, they may not even list the company—they may sell directly to a known buyer, often within the same network. At every stage, visibility is minimised to preserve optionality, reduce competition, and avoid external pressure.

It's important to recognise that this approach is not about secrecy for its own sake. It's about *control over narrative and timing.* Public moves invite speculation, headlines, and scrutiny. Quiet moves preserve clarity and room to manoeuvre. A sudden divestment from a volatile sector can tank the value of held assets if done publicly. A well-timed quiet exit, conducted through private placement or secondary markets, avoids signalling and allows the holder to exit at fair value. Likewise, a high-profile investment in an emerging industry can attract competitors, inflate valuations, or trigger premature regulatory attention. A small, silent allocation through a specialist fund avoids all of the above.

Reputation also plays a crucial role. For wealthy individuals and families, reputational capital often outweighs financial capital in strategic decisions. The public visibility of a failed investment, controversial partnership, or abrupt exit can carry costs far beyond the balance sheet. Quiet moves mitigate these reputational risks. They allow investors to reposition themselves without explanation, recalibrate without defensiveness, and distance themselves from volatility without fanfare. This is especially important in sectors like media, biotechnology, or emerging technologies, where public sentiment shifts rapidly and visibility can quickly become a liability.

Yet perhaps the most subtle—and misunderstood—advantage of quiet moves lies in their *emotional leverage.* Those operating outside these networks are often forced to act under pressure, respond to volatility in real time, and carry the psychological burden of incomplete information. The wealthy, protected by their networks and timing privileges, act from a position of *calm.* They are less reactive, less susceptible to panic, and less exposed to groupthink. When others are scrambling, they are often already repositioned. When others are euphoric, they are already exiting. This discipline is not simply individual temperament—it is enabled by *informational and relational insulation.*

This insulation is not evenly distributed. The ability to make quiet moves depends on access—access to advisers, legal architects, tax specialists, private bankers, and other nodes in a web of privileged intelligence. It also requires *trust capital*—a history of acting with discretion, honouring soft agreements, and delivering value without extraction. In elite circles, one's ability to keep a move quiet is often more valuable than one's ability to execute it boldly. Trust is the gatekeeper of opportunity. Discretion is its currency.

It is worth noting, too, that the infrastructure of quiet moves is rarely visible in public data. No amount of studying ETF flows, public filings, or headline coverage will reveal what is being quietly restructured, slowly exited, or delicately hedged behind the scenes. The informational asymmetry here is not about technology or analytics—it's about *who gets the call before the market does*. That call doesn't show up in the charts. But it often determines who absorbs losses and who sidesteps them.

What is often mistaken as elite intuition is in fact engineered advantage. The wealthiest are not simply luckier or braver. They are structurally positioned to *see things earlier, move more quietly, and act more selectively*. Their success lies not in public signals, but in quiet ones—in the murmurs at trusted tables, the memos circulated privately, the soft signals of shifts yet to be priced.

For those outside these networks, this reality can feel alienating. But it also reveals what *can* be studied and, to a degree, emulated. The concept of quiet moves invites a different kind of financial literacy—one that pays attention not to noise, but to *who isn't speaking and why*. It urges us to think in terms of optionality, discretion, relational capital, and the invisible structures that define real advantage. Because in the architecture of enduring wealth, what we *don't* see often matters more than what we do.

Chapter 2
The Inheritance of Intelligence

Wealth, contrary to common perception, is rarely sustained merely through inheritance of capital. What endures across generations is far more subtle: the mental infrastructure that governs how money is perceived, managed, and protected. The truly wealthy inherit frameworks for interacting with capital—mental scaffolds that shape decisions on risk, control, scarcity, stewardship, and responsibility. While many receive financial literacy in the form of definitions, ratios, or investment heuristics, enduring wealth is built on the transmission of judgment itself. This quiet architecture—the invisible systems behind behaviour—is what separates fortunes that evaporate within a few decades from those that compound, adapt, and insulate against volatility.

Public discourse on inheritance often obsesses over numbers: the amount, the timing, the legal structures. These questions, though important, are secondary. The more decisive factor is philosophical: which beliefs and mental models are passed down alongside the balance sheet? What assumptions about the purpose of money, ownership, and obligation inform the decisions of the next generation? When a young heir confronts market turbulence, litigation, or a generational transition, it is not textbook knowledge that preserves the capital—it is internalised judgement, cultivated through deliberate exposure to risk and structured decision-making.

This transmission of intelligence is rarely accidental. In high-net-worth families that successfully preserve wealth, one finds intentional frameworks: legal mechanisms, trust structures, and perhaps most importantly, training environments in which financial complexity is introduced gradually, alongside emotional conditioning. Children are not simply instructed on how to spend or invest; they are taught to engage with uncertainty, given controlled exposure to consequences, and allowed to build capacity to manage real assets without imperilling the system.

Contrast this with the familiar pattern of wealth dissipation: earning, spending, and dissolution. Across cultures, this pattern is codified in sayings: in the West, "shirtsleeves to shirtsleeves in three generations"; in Japan, "rice paddies to rice paddies"; in China, "wealth does not survive three generations." The thread linking these patterns is not a moral failing, but a deficit in durable thinking. The first generation labours for capital, the second enjoys it, and the third inherits entitlement without the cognitive tools to safeguard it.

The Rockefeller family exemplifies the alternative. Their fortune was among the first in America consciously structured for multi-generational continuity. John D. Rockefeller's heirs were not simply beneficiaries of trusts—they were embedded in a deliberate institutional legacy. The family office was a tool not only for investment management, but for cultivating discipline: overseeing philanthropy, establishing governance norms, coordinating decision-making, and controlling the flow of information. Family councils provided rhythm and collective engagement. These mechanisms did not eliminate dysfunction, but channelled it through durable structures that protected the capital from internal entropy.

The genius of this approach lay not in locking up money in complex arrangements, but in encoding judgement. The system transmitted decision-making frameworks: how to balance risk, pursue measured experimentation, and deploy capital thoughtfully. These were containers—spaces in which heirs could operate without exposing themselves to financial ruin from inexperience or ego.

Training in these environments begins early, often not through formal economics lessons, but through exposure to core concepts: liquidity versus net worth, control versus ownership, long-term versus short-term orientation, resilience versus raw performance. A child might learn why borrowing against assets is preferable to liquidating them, or why allocation decisions are about optionality and timing rather than returns alone. They may manage a small donor-advised fund before being entrusted with larger portfolios. These exercises are rehearsals for agency: teaching the next generation that capital is not merely a store of value, but a force to be directed, contained, and deployed judiciously.

There is a stark difference between knowing financial language and possessing financial immunity. Many financially literate individuals are nonetheless fragile: versed in compound interest and asset classes, yet overexposed or dependent on a single income stream. When shocks occur—markets seize, liquidity dries, legal challenges arise—they are unprotected. Financial literacy without insulation is like understanding the mechanics of a car engine without knowing how to drive defensively. Knowledge alone is insufficient; positional understanding is required.

Enduring wealth is taught differently. Heirs are trained to assess their place within complex systems, recognise which variables they can influence, and act to preserve principal and optionality. Optionality—the capacity to wait, observe, and act from strength rather than reaction—is central. Families that cultivate this mindset do not chase every opportunity; they maintain the freedom to choose, acquiring assets opportunistically in downturns, exiting disputes gracefully, and pivoting through regulatory or structural changes when necessary. This is agility in the service of survival.

All of this—early conditioning, structural learning, mental frameworks—constitutes the inheritance of intelligence. It is not a mystical gift, nor mere IQ, insider networks, or elite schooling, though those may assist. It is the deliberate cultivation of interpretive depth: the ability to read environments, act judiciously under uncertainty, and shield capital from emotional, social, or reputational erosion.

These systems are largely invisible. Publicly, one sees family names on buildings, philanthropic foundations, or art collections. What is hidden are the Wednesday morning governance calls, the quiet interventions when an heir strays, the structured timelines for control transitions, the meticulously refined values statements, and the apprenticeship embedded in boards or philanthropic endeavours. These are the mechanisms of intelligence transmission: understated, iterative, and cumulative.

Reconceiving wealth in these terms expands the very definition of capital. It is not merely assets or liquidity; it is structure, insight, patience, and mental resilience under pressure. Families who grasp this redefine inheritance: it is not simply to endow, but to equip.

Because capital without judgement is exposed, and judgement without structure is fragile.

The inheritance of intelligence is the ultimate insulation. It allows wealth to adapt without fracturing, absorbs shocks without descending into litigation or dissolution, and converts what might otherwise be a single-generation performance into a multi-generational strategy. Recognising this shifts the view of capital from static gift to evolving bequest—a starting position demanding increasing sophistication as it compounds.

Not Just Money: Passing Down Thinking Models

What separates enduring wealth from transient fortune is rarely found in financial statements. It is found in the *thinking patterns* passed quietly from one generation to the next—patterns that govern how individuals relate to money, perceive risk, interpret scarcity, and define agency. High-net-worth families who succeed across generations do not merely transfer assets; they transfer *interpretive frameworks*. These frameworks shape how heirs respond under pressure, how they assess opportunity, and how they make decisions that affect not just their capital, but their character. Wealth that lasts is not just resourced—it is *mentally rehearsed.*

To understand this, one must start by abandoning the idea that financial legacy is solely about monetary provision. A bequest without a worldview is an inheritance without orientation. It leaves the recipient with means, but no method—wealth, but no *mental map* for navigating it. And unlike money, which can be tracked, taxed, and divided, mental models are more elusive. They are coded into behaviour, revealed in language, reinforced through exposure. A wealthy parent may never explicitly teach their child how to think about cash flow or leverage. But through observation—how the parent responds to volatility, what they prioritise in conversation, how they allocate time and energy—the child absorbs a worldview. These cues are subtle, but cumulative. Over time, they shape what the child comes to regard as normal, prudent, or risky.

One of the most consistent features of families who preserve wealth over time is their *deliberate modelling of decision-making under uncertainty.* They don't just explain outcomes; they explain *why a decision was made, what variables were considered, what was deemed unknowable, and how trade-offs were weighed.* These aren't financial lessons—they are *thinking lessons*, often delivered in the cadence of daily life. At the dinner table, a father casually discusses why he passed on a lucrative deal because the counterparty lacked governance discipline. A mother walks her daughter through the consequences of extending payment terms to a client with cash flow issues. These aren't theoretical lectures. They are moments of *thinking in real time*—and for the child, they become a library of case studies, rich with nuance.

Scarcity, too, is taught not by amount, but by *frame.* A child can grow up surrounded by wealth yet internalise a disciplined view of resource allocation if scarcity is reframed as a constraint on *attention, time, or reputation*, rather than on money alone. The problem with many failed successions is not that the heirs lacked exposure to wealth—it's that they lacked exposure to *restraint.* They were given access to capital without ever seeing how capital is *constrained*—by timing, by ethics, by long-term vision. In this sense, the critical mental model is not frugality—it is *strategic resource stewardship.* This reframing immunises heirs from both indulgence and panic. It allows them to move with calm when others are reactive and to say no when others are seduced.

The emphasis on agency is equally vital. In resilient families, wealth is framed not as a prize, but as a *responsibility.* This is not rhetorical. It manifests in how children are involved in philanthropic decisions, in the degree to which they are encouraged to challenge family investment theses, and in how failure is handled. If a child is allowed to fail early—within controlled financial contexts, with debrief and reflection—they learn that agency includes error and recovery, not just control and dominance. This kind of exposure builds decision-making muscles that compound over time. Agency is not the power to act freely; it is the *capacity to act wisely when stakes are real.*

In families where these thinking models are neglected, the results are often predictable. The second or third generation inherits financial capital but not decision fluency. They lack the schema to detect bad deals, to resist lifestyle inflation, or to anticipate systemic shocks. They confuse liquidity with strength, risk-taking with courage, consumption with confidence. They may be financially literate in the narrow sense—capable of reading balance sheets, fluent in yield curves—but ill-equipped to manage complexity. Without embedded thinking models, wealth becomes performative. And performative wealth is fragile by design.

The families that escape this fate often do so through a *deliberate architecture of exposure*. They do not hand their children full control over capital in early adulthood. Instead, they create graduated environments—donor-advised funds, simulated investment portfolios, junior family board roles—that expose heirs to decision-making without catastrophic risk. This staged exposure mimics the mental pattern-building of professional athletes or military officers: pressure is applied gradually, under supervision, with increasing consequence. The goal is not immediate mastery—it is *mental adaptation to feedback under complexity*.

A particularly useful distinction in this context is between *abstract literacy* and *contextual fluency*. The former is what most financial education offers: terms, formulas, structures. The latter is what thinking models produce: a nuanced sense of timing, context, and emotional equilibrium. A child who is merely taught that diversification is prudent may still over-concentrate in tech stocks. A child who has observed how capital behaves differently across cycles—and how concentration creates fragility—will treat diversification not as a principle, but as a *discipline*. The difference is not knowledge. It is *thinking architecture*.

This thinking architecture often includes philosophical dimensions that go beyond economics. It asks: What is the purpose of money? What constitutes enough? What do we owe to others? These questions are not indulgent. They are *boundary-setting mechanisms*. In the absence of philosophical clarity, wealth becomes self-referential—used to chase ever-larger returns, status markers, or control. But with a well-formed philosophical base, families can align decisions with identity, not just outcome. This alignment reduces conflict, strengthens cohesion, and improves strategic clarity. The most sophisticated family offices are often as focused on *values articulation* as they are on asset allocation. They understand that *internal clarity reduces external confusion.*

It is also worth noting that thinking models are most powerful when they are *transparent but flexible.* The best families do not indoctrinate. They invite reflection. They allow younger members to challenge old frameworks, propose new models, and bring in outside expertise. What remains consistent is not the content of thought, but the *rigour of thinking.* This intellectual seriousness, transmitted across generations, becomes a form of cultural capital—one that protects the family from both internal drift and external seduction.

In sum, the most valuable inheritance is not a trust fund, a property portfolio, or a business stake. It is the *internal compass* that governs how these resources are understood, protected, and deployed. It is the mental calibration that helps an individual know when to act, when to wait, and when to walk away. It is the inherited capacity to remain clear-eyed when complexity rises and to recognise that wealth is not just a number—it is a *force that must be directed, not consumed.* The families who understand this pass down something far more durable than riches. They pass down *resilience of judgement.* And that, in the long arc of history, is what truly lasts.

Case Study: The Rockefeller Playbook

It is one of the rarest feats in financial history: transforming the proceeds of a single lifetime into a multigenerational, systematised engine of influence and preservation. The Rockefeller name has become synonymous not merely with wealth, but with the architecture of wealth that *lasts.* To study the Rockefeller family is not to gawk at fortune, but to understand the infrastructure that protects, extends, and institutionalises it. For over a century, their capital has endured world wars, economic depressions, currency debasements, and massive shifts in political sentiment. The core question is not how they made their money—John D. Rockefeller's monopoly on oil through Standard Oil is well-trodden historical ground—but how they designed *to keep it.* The answer lies in a confluence of design disciplines: legal structures, governance protocols, institutional habits, and cultural frameworks, all orchestrated to manage *more than assets*. The Rockefeller playbook is, above all, a manual in managing *complexity across time.*

When John D. Rockefeller began formalising the structures that would protect his wealth, he was responding to a problem few had yet encountered at that scale: how do you prevent inherited money from becoming a liability? How do you separate capital from ego, distribute power without diffusion, and instil restraint in a context of abundance? These questions were not answered through passive investment vehicles or wishful thinking. They were answered through the formation of what is now considered one of the earliest modern family offices: a purpose-built entity to manage not only the assets of a family, but the coordination, education, legal affairs, tax optimisation, and philanthropic agendas of its members.

The family office was established in 1882—an era long before the term "private wealth management" became an industry. Its purpose was clear: provide centralised financial stewardship while insulating individual members from the burden and risk of directly managing vast sums. This move was not merely operational—it was philosophical. Rockefeller understood that the diffusion of decision-making across uninformed or emotionally reactive heirs could lead to asset depletion. By placing a professional intermediary between the capital and its inheritors, he introduced *deliberate friction*—a system in which access was governed by rules, not sentiment. This friction is a recurring theme in wealth preservation: the wise constraint of access is not a limitation but a design choice. Friction disciplines behaviour.

Within this office, Rockefeller embedded another core principle: *information asymmetry within the family must be reduced.* As the family grew—in size, geography, and complexity—so did the potential for misalignment. The office functioned not just as an asset manager but as a communication nexus. It hosted regular meetings, circulated reports, maintained archives, and provided a shared factual substrate upon which the family could make decisions. This coordination mechanism was critical in maintaining strategic coherence across generations. Without it, inherited wealth fragments. With it, it compounds.

But governance is not merely about sharing information. It is about managing *power*. The Rockefeller family addressed this with a multi-layered model of representation and voting. Committees were formed. Philanthropic decisions were deliberated upon. Different branches of the family had defined roles in strategic planning. This structure had a twofold effect: it preserved cohesion by giving members a voice, and it limited destabilisation by ensuring that no single individual could override the system. It wasn't democracy in the populist sense. It was *governed inclusion*—participation without dilution of control.

The role of philanthropy within this model deserves special attention. The Rockefeller Foundation, established in 1913, was not simply a charitable entity. It was a *strategic extension* of the family's influence and a training ground for the younger generation. Family members were often brought into foundation work before being given oversight of private investment vehicles. This sequencing was not accidental. It served two critical functions: first, to build a moral and strategic consciousness around wealth; second, to provide real-world exposure to governance processes, stakeholder management, and strategic giving. Through this exposure, heirs learned how to think in systems, not just in transactions. They were not only taught *what* to give, but *how* to think about impact, longevity, and public perception. Philanthropy was not a reputational afterthought. It was a mechanism for continuity.

Trust structures were also central to the Rockefeller playbook. These were not static repositories of wealth, but *dynamic governance tools*. Assets were held in a series of interconnected trusts, often designed to isolate risk, manage tax exposure, and enforce conditional disbursements. Crucially, these trusts were drafted with enough flexibility to adapt to changing tax codes and market conditions, while preserving the founder's intentions. Legal elasticity with philosophical fidelity—that was the design brief. The result was a set of instruments that shielded capital from impulsive withdrawals, marital disputes, or opportunistic claimants, without becoming brittle or obsolete.

This legal sophistication extended into asset strategy. The Rockefeller family office diversified early and often—into real estate, natural resources, private equity, and public markets—while maintaining a commitment to low leverage and high liquidity buffers. This posture wasn't glamorous, but it was resilient. It reflected a core tenet of the family's philosophy: *capital must be positioned to withstand shocks, not merely to maximise yield.* In this respect, the Rockefeller portfolio resembled a well-capitalised institution more than a risk-seeking investor. It prioritised optionality over optimisation.

Optionality also defined the family's approach to succession. Unlike many dynastic fortunes that deteriorate under contested inheritances or ill-prepared heirs, the Rockefellers invested heavily in education, mentorship, and staged responsibility. Members of the younger generation were not given immediate access to large sums. Instead, they were placed on governance boards, engaged in joint ventures, or supported in entrepreneurial initiatives with defined risk envelopes. Capital was released *with context,* not merely as entitlement. This developmental pathway created leaders who could engage with complexity without being consumed by it. The implicit message was clear: *wealth requires stewardship, not simply enjoyment.*

That stewardship mindset was reinforced by norms—often unwritten but deeply embedded. Displays of extravagance were discouraged. Professional excellence was celebrated over financial showboating. Visibility was managed with care. This was not a public relations strategy. It was a cultural inoculation against entitlement and reputational fragility. Families who survive over centuries do so not because they accumulate more, but because they *signal less.* The Rockefeller name became durable not because it was everywhere, but because it was *guarded.* That restraint was cultural capital in its own right.

One of the most misunderstood elements of the Rockefeller system is that it was *not immune to conflict.* There were disagreements, divorces, public criticisms, and political scrutiny. But what distinguished the family was not the absence of disorder—it was the presence of *containers for it.* Disputes were mediated within structured forums. Dissent was anticipated. The system was designed with slack and redundancy. Just as engineering systems require tolerance margins to absorb strain, family wealth structures require *dispute bandwidth* to preserve coherence under duress.

For contemporary families seeking to emulate the Rockefeller model, the takeaway is not to copy structures blindly. It is to internalise a principle: *governance is the compound interest of wealth.* Just as early financial discipline yields exponential financial growth, early governance discipline yields generational coherence. It reduces entropy, builds trust, and embeds values into operations. Whether through a family office, a shared investment vehicle, or a philanthropic entity, the Rockefeller approach insists on one idea: wealth is not static—it is *systemic.* If it is not actively designed, it will passively dissipate.

The Rockefeller playbook, then, is not a monument to financial excess. It is a blueprint for engineered resilience. It reminds us that money does not preserve itself, that institutions must be built before they are needed, and that *capital without coordination is merely liquidity in waiting.* To understand dynastic wealth, one must look not just at what is held, but at how it is held—*and by whom, with what constraints, and under what philosophy.* The Rockefeller legacy survives not because of what they earned, but because of how they *structured what they refused to lose.*

The Training Begins Early

Children born into wealth are not born understanding it. They arrive with no innate ability to navigate liquidity, manage asymmetric risks, or comprehend the subtle difference between control and ownership. What they do absorb—if they are to preserve and extend what they inherit—must be taught. Not through lectures or lectures masquerading as life lessons, but through *embedded training systems* that begin well before the child is legally entitled to make financial decisions. In families where wealth endures, this early training does not focus on consumption, privilege, or even technical finance. It focuses on *stewardship*—on cultivating the internal frameworks required to think about capital as a responsibility that must be carried forward, not simply enjoyed.

This distinction is fundamental. Consumption is reactive. It is concerned with access, comfort, and the aesthetics of wealth. Stewardship is proactive. It requires the child to see the family's capital not as a personal resource, but as an asset base that must be maintained, protected, and used strategically. The child is not the centre of the wealth. They are a *participant in its continuity*. And this reframing—subtle but profound—shapes behaviours decades before any financial event appears on a balance sheet.

What separates high-functioning financial families from those who devolve into intergenerational fragility is not the size of the inheritance, but the *timing and quality of exposure*. Children who are never exposed to risk, ambiguity, or financial consequence often reach adulthood with no capacity to understand volatility. Conversely, families that begin building these capacities early—through controlled, real-world experiences—equip their heirs with the judgement that textbooks and advisory briefings cannot provide.

Take the example of philanthropic involvement. In many dynastic families, a child's first exposure to financial agency is through the family's foundation. They may be given a junior role on a grant committee, asked to make a funding recommendation, or assigned the task of evaluating potential outcomes for a small donation. On paper, these are minor engagements. But in practice, they are *early labs for capital deployment*. The child learns to balance purpose with outcome, to assess the trade-offs between competing priorities, and to understand that money—even when used altruistically—must be directed with clarity. These early exposures train not only analytical skills, but *values-based decision-making under constraint*.

This approach extends into how wealth is discussed—if it is discussed at all. In families with enduring capital, conversations about money begin before wealth becomes a legal reality. But they are not framed in terms of net worth or entitlement. Instead, they focus on *what money is for*. Is it for freedom? Is it for impact? Is it for preservation? These conversations do not indoctrinate—they orient. They create an early sense that wealth must be understood *in context*, that it is not absolute, and that its meaning is as much moral as it is financial. Children learn that money does not solve problems automatically. It introduces new ones. And unless it is managed with foresight, it often becomes a source of noise rather than clarity.

Families that take this seriously often design formal training structures. These can include family charters, educational tracks, investment committees with staggered access, or simulated decision-making exercises. A 15-year-old might be assigned a mock portfolio to manage and report on. An 18-year-old may be asked to assess the risk of a hypothetical venture capital allocation. These are not games. They are early inoculations against the allure of momentum thinking, herd behaviour, and emotional misjudgement—traits that market stress will ruthlessly expose if left untrained. The objective is not mastery. It is *judgement under mild pressure*, so that when real pressure arrives, the mental reflexes already exist.

Critically, this training does not require a precocious interest in finance. It requires only consistent exposure to *how decisions are made*, and why. When a parent declines an investment opportunity, the child is told not just the outcome, but the reasoning. When a trust is structured with a delayed distribution clause, the logic is explained—not merely as a rule, but as an act of care. Over time, the child internalises a sense that wealth is not simply inherited; it is *curated across time*. It must be defended from entropy, both external and internal.

This is especially important during periods of economic turbulence. In moments of crisis—when asset prices crash, liquidity tightens, or institutions become unreliable—stewardship-trained heirs do not react as consumers or beneficiaries. They react as *position managers*. They understand the difference between a temporary drawdown and a structural impairment. They know when to pause and when to act. They resist the emotional urge to exit prematurely or pursue yield too aggressively. This behavioural insulation is what separates families who emerge intact from those who self-liquidate under pressure. It is not an accident. It is the result of mental conditioning that began *before the headlines turned red.*

The contrast becomes most visible when you look at families who did *not* undertake this training. Children raised in environments where wealth is either taboo or taken for granted often fall into one of two traps: disengagement or entitlement. The disengaged heir treats capital as an abstraction—something to be ignored until it disappears. The entitled heir treats it as fuel for personal expression—something to be consumed, flaunted, or used to shortcut the hard parts of adulthood. Neither position is sustainable.

Both lead to fragility. What's missing is not financial acumen, but *ownership of thought*. Without it, the inheritance becomes a volatile asset—amplifying the consequences of every poor decision.

To prevent this, some families go so far as to introduce heirs to *family governance structures* before they have voting rights. They are invited to observe, to listen, to ask questions. In doing so, they gain fluency in the norms, expectations, and tensions that accompany collective capital management. They see that wealth is not just about individual choice. It is also about *coordinated constraint*. They learn to negotiate, to compromise, to weigh long-term cohesion over short-term wins. These skills are not innate. They are the product of *deliberate cultural engineering*.

What this ultimately reinforces is that early training is not a tactical advantage—it is a *defensive necessity*. In a world of increasing complexity, where regulatory environments shift and asset classes behave unpredictably, the next generation cannot be expected to navigate risk competently without having first *experienced calibrated doses of it*. And yet, many families defer this responsibility, believing that competence will emerge naturally when the time comes. It doesn't. Competence must be *built under load*. The earlier that load is introduced—appropriately scaled—the more resilient the decision-maker becomes.

To put it plainly: money without stewardship training is not a gift. It is exposure. And the earlier that stewardship is taught—not through speeches, but through *participation*—the stronger the family's capital position becomes over time. This is not about raising financial prodigies. It is about raising *responsible inheritors* who understand that wealth, if misused, becomes a corrosive force—but if stewarded wisely, becomes a generative one. The training, then, is not just about what the child will *do* with the money. It is about who they must *become* in order to deserve it.

Financial Literacy ≠ Financial Immunity

A person can recite the definitions of compounding interest, know the difference between equities and bonds, or model discounted cash flows with elegant precision—and still be economically fragile. This is not a paradox. It is the misapprehension at the heart of countless well-meaning financial education efforts. *Knowing* financial language is not the same as *being insulated* from financial damage. In fact, a surplus of knowledge without corresponding insulation can lead to overconfidence—an intellectual fluency that masks vulnerability. True financial resilience is not a matter of vocabulary. It is a matter of structure, positioning, and behavioural discipline under stress.

Financial literacy has become a catch-all solution in policy circles and personal finance circles alike. It is assumed that if individuals simply understand key concepts—interest rates, budgeting, credit scores—they will make better decisions, build security, and escape cycles of volatility. But this assumption presumes a level playing field where knowledge is the missing ingredient. It is not. In many cases, the *application* of knowledge is constrained by factors far outside the individual's control: volatility of income, absence of capital buffers, lack of institutional access, or exposure to systemic risk. One can know exactly what not to do and still be forced to do it.

Consider a highly educated professional who understands portfolio diversification, asset allocation, and the logic of emergency funds. If that individual experiences a health crisis, a lawsuit, or the sudden loss of employment—without pre-existing buffers—they may have no choice but to liquidate retirement savings at a penalty, take on expensive debt, or default on obligations. The issue was never ignorance. It was *exposure without insulation.*

By contrast, insulation is the invisible infrastructure that allows the wealthy to experience the same macroeconomic events *differently.* Insulation is not merely cash reserves, though those matter. It includes legal entities that separate liability from ownership. It includes diversified income streams that reduce reliance on any one employer, client, or market. It includes pre-negotiated access to credit lines that provide liquidity when banks become cautious. It includes proactive advisory teams who identify potential risks before they become visible to the average investor. Insulation is *not about predicting outcomes.* It is about *buffering fragility.*

One of the least discussed dimensions of insulation is temporal: the wealthy can *wait.* When the market crashes or a deal goes sideways, they are not forced to liquidate assets to meet short-term obligations. This ability to sit through volatility—to let cycles complete without panic—translates into structural advantages that compound over time. Financial literacy alone does not produce this patience. Only insulation can buy time at scale. And time, in capital terms, is often the most decisive asset.

There is also an emotional component to immunity. People under financial stress make different decisions. They become more reactive, more conservative, or more prone to desperation. The wealthy, by being insulated from daily volatility, can remain more dispassionate in their analysis and more deliberate in their movements. This is often mistaken for superior intelligence. It is not. It is *decision-making under reduced pressure*, which yields better outcomes not because the person is smarter, but because their environment is less adversarial.

The real danger in conflating literacy with immunity is that it breeds a false sense of preparedness. A middle-class investor who has read financial books, listens to market podcasts, and runs spreadsheets may feel confident in their positioning—until an event exposes the structural limits of their setup. They learn, painfully, that understanding asset classes is not the same as having *access* to protective vehicles like family trusts, offshore structures, or tailored insurance products. They realise that resilience is not what they *know*, but what they *hold*, how it is protected, and whether they can afford to act slowly.

This is why high-net-worth families invest less in teaching financial trivia and more in embedding *thinking frameworks*. Rather than emphasising tactics ("buy low, sell high"), they model how to evaluate systemic risk, how to assess counterparty exposure, how to analyse legal positioning. These frameworks are not about optimising yield. They are about *reducing fragility over time*. Immunity, in this context, means having the capacity to absorb shocks without behaviourally or structurally collapsing.

It also explains why the wealthy often spend considerable resources on advice. Not because they lack basic literacy, but because they understand that insulation is a *dynamic condition.* What worked last year may not protect this year. Tax codes change, regulatory arbitrage windows close, geopolitical events reprice assumptions. To stay insulated requires constant reevaluation, much of it delegated to professionals whose job is not to educate the principal but to *pre-empt fragility on their behalf.* The wealthy are not seeking to become more literate. They are seeking to remain protected.

This creates a social asymmetry. In public discourse, literacy is democratised, even evangelised. Insulation is whispered, gatekept, or hidden entirely. One can easily find free courses on budgeting or passive investing. Far fewer people know how to establish a dynasty trust or construct an LLC cascade that separates liability from asset ownership. Not because the information is secret, but because it is *contextually inaccessible.* It only becomes relevant when the scale and structure of one's wealth demands it.

Moreover, insulation is cumulative. The more one has, the easier it is to create more. Once a protective layer is in place—say, through a family office or legal shield—it becomes easier to take calculated risks, enter private deals, or make longer-term bets. These risks are not perceived as risky in the same way, because *downside is bounded.* And once downside is bounded, decision-making shifts fundamentally. The wealthy can afford to be aggressive without courting ruin. The middle class, by contrast, often cannot afford to make a single major error.

This distinction matters because it reorients where we place emphasis. The public obsession with literacy should not be abandoned. But it must be *reframed.* Teaching people to understand credit is not enough if their cost of capital is structurally higher. Teaching them about diversification is not enough if their only investment options are limited to public markets. True empowerment must include *access to insulation tools*, or at minimum, *a clear-eyed understanding of their absence.*

In this light, the conversation shifts from personal responsibility to systemic positioning. Not in a defeatist sense, but in a way that enables individuals to *build the layers of insulation available to them*. These may be modest at first—such as building liquidity buffers, diversifying income sources, or formalising business protections—but they matter. Because over time, they create the capacity to act with calm rather than panic, with intention rather than compulsion.

The lesson here is clear: *literacy without insulation is exposure*. It creates the illusion of control without the substance of protection. And the remedy is not to abandon education, but to integrate it with structural awareness—of what shields exist, how they are constructed, and why they matter when stress inevitably arrives. Because wealth is not sustained by knowing what an ETF is. It is sustained by *never needing to sell one in a crisis*.

Chapter 3
Liquidity Is Leverage

A high net worth, in isolation, tells us little when obligations arrive faster than capital can be mobilised. In the practical economy, wealth that cannot be converted—smoothly, strategically, and immediately—into usable cash is often a liability rather than an asset. Across cycles of boom and bust, it is rarely portfolio size that separates the solvent from the overextended; it is liquidity—the capacity to access capital without incurring loss, penalty, or reputational fallout. Among the financially sophisticated, liquidity is not an afterthought or a safety net. It is the centrepiece of resilience, cultivated deliberately. To grasp how the wealthy preserve and expand their advantage, we must think of liquidity not as inconvenience but as a tool of power.

Popular mythology equates wealth with high-value holdings: sprawling estates, stakes in private companies, rare art, jewellery, or private equity. Yet these are largely illiquid positions. Designed for appreciation or prestige rather than manoeuvrability, they become hostage to market conditions when conditions sour. The discrepancy between perceived and functional wealth is stark: someone with modest paper value but ample liquid buffers often fares far better in a downturn than a magnate ensnared by immovable assets.

This asymmetry is clearest in moments of stress. During the 2008 financial crisis, institutions failed not because they lacked assets but because they lacked cash. The lesson applies equally at the household level. Those holding "dry powder"—uncommitted cash ready to deploy—were not only protected but empowered. They acquired distressed assets, renegotiated terms, or simply waited. Waiting itself becomes an advantage when the rest are forced to act prematurely. Liquidity is, therefore, active leverage, not passive protection.

Among the ultra-wealthy, liquidity is instinctive and institutionalised. Family offices and advisers treat it as central to the architecture of wealth. It is measured across time horizons, asset classes, jurisdictions, and counterparty exposure. A common rule among sophisticated investors is simple: if you cannot access it without a haircut, it is not liquid. If it cannot be drawn in the right currency, under suitable tax conditions, and with legal clarity, it is effectively unusable in a crisis.

It is crucial to distinguish liquidity from cash. Hundreds of millions in a fund with withdrawal gates, pledged collateral, or foreign controls may as well be trapped. True liquidity consists of unencumbered, callable capital—cash ready to act without strings, often lying dormant until opportunity demands deployment.

This patient capital is frequently misunderstood by those outside these circles. Why hold idle money when it could be earning? Why accept a sub-inflation yield? The answer is optionality. Liquidity does not generate immediate return, but it unlocks outsized gains when others are illiquid and desperate. It allows one to dictate terms, acquire assets at discount, and negotiate from strength. This philosophy—waiting strategically—is learned, not innate. It requires resisting the instinct to deploy capital for the sake of activity.

The wealthy also structure holdings to maintain functional liquidity even while appearing asset-heavy. Rather than direct ownership, they rely on trusts, holding companies, partnerships, and layered entities. Control is retained while exposure is compartmentalised. Assets can be sold, reassigned, or borrowed against without disturbing the broader portfolio. Liquidity becomes structural, not incidental.

This architecture also supports selective opacity. By controlling assets indirectly, the wealthy insulate themselves from liability, reputational risk, or premature disclosure. Strategic flexibility—repositioning holdings quietly—is as valuable as cash itself. In a downturn, this allows them to retreat or redeploy silently, contrasting sharply with those forced into visible fire sales. Liquidity, therefore, extends into informational advantage.

History offers stark examples. In 2008, the headlines fixated on the failures. Yet behind the scenes were families and funds who lost little to nothing—not due to prescience but because exposure was managed. Short-term treasuries rather than long-term real estate, exits from overheated markets months before the crash, and discretionary capital ready to acquire distressed debt or trophy assets:

these were the advantages of patient design. Calm is built, not coincidental.

In buoyant markets, it is tempting to ignore these lessons. Credit is cheap, prices rise, and liquidity feels optional. Yet the cost of illiquidity is measured under stress, not normalcy. Those who endure are rarely the boldest; they are the best positioned. Liquidity, then, is more than a hedge—it is a philosophy, a lens that treats cycles not as surprises but as certainties requiring preparation.

For those constructing wealth architectures—entrepreneurs, investors, or professionals—the question is not "What is my net worth?" but "How much can I deploy without panic, penalty, or permission?" The answer is often smaller than assumed. Wealth is not diminished by this discipline; it is clarified. Control is made visible, room to manoeuvre is preserved, and constraints under pressure are anticipated. Liquidity is not avoidance of risk; it is creation of space to act when risk becomes real.

This chapter begins with that principle: liquidity is leverage. Not in the financial-engineering sense, but in the most fundamental: it multiplies discretion, patience, and power. Without it, even enormous wealth becomes brittle; with it, modest wealth can scale. The following chapters will explore how this leverage is constructed, protected, and applied by those who refuse to be constrained by the apparent size of their balance sheets.

Why Cash Flow Matters More Than Net Worth

Wealth, as popularly understood, is often a fiction of accounting. The public eye obsesses over balance sheets, headline valuations, and high-net-worth rankings, treating them as reliable proxies for financial power. Yet among the truly enduring rich—those who survive crises without liquidation, reputation loss, or diminished influence—wealth is not measured in what one owns, but in what one can move. *Liquidity is the quiet engine of resilience*, and its strategic importance is nowhere more pronounced than during periods of economic disruption.

Consider this: during the 2008 financial crisis, more than one hundred publicly listed billionaires saw their net worth halved within months. But a different cohort—less visible, less leveraged, and far more liquid—weathered the storm with little public notice and extraordinary advantage. The difference lay not in their access to opportunity or the size of their portfolios, but in the structural agility provided by cash flow. *Net worth is static; cash flow is kinetic. And in times of stress, only the latter buys freedom.*

The cultural fixation on being "rich on paper" is, in part, a function of the middle-class financial imagination. Valuation—be it of a home, a stock holding, or a start-up—is aspirational. It promises future access, even if that access is contingent, illiquid, or volatile. It comforts us with numbers that signal affluence while obscuring fragility. But to the structurally rich, valuation is not a goal; it is a tool. And its utility is only as strong as the liquidity that supports it.

Liquidity, in this context, is not merely "having cash." It is *having control over deployable capital without penalty*. It is the ability to pause, manoeuvre, and act in real-time without forced conversion or distressed exits. This includes untapped lines of credit, strategically timed capital calls, reinsurance float, or capital reserves embedded within trust structures. It also means *access to capital without signalling distress*—a critical distinction that separates those who can move quietly from those who must explain their moves publicly.

The mass-market misunderstanding of liquidity is evident in personal finance advice, which often conflates emergency funds with strategic flexibility. A middle-income family is advised to maintain three to six months of expenses in cash, primarily for emergencies. In contrast, high-net-worth individuals and family offices maintain *dry powder*—uncommitted, nimble capital—not for emergencies, but for *advantage*. The logic is inverse: while the middle class builds liquidity to survive downturns, the wealthy maintain liquidity to exploit them.

During the depths of the 2008 crisis, Warren Buffett secured preferential terms in his deals with Goldman Sachs and General Electric, not because of his net worth, but because of his liquidity. He could act swiftly, offer capital when others could not, and demand returns that would be inaccessible in normal markets. This is *opportunistic liquidity*, a posture reserved for those who are not merely solvent, but strategically patient.

The strategic discipline of maintaining liquidity often demands resisting the seduction of yield. Many investors chase high returns by tying up capital in long-duration or illiquid assets—private equity, real estate, venture capital—without understanding the cost of illiquidity. What looks profitable in boom times becomes brittle when the economic cycle turns. By contrast, sophisticated families often allocate a portion of their capital not to maximise gains, but to *minimise dependency*. This requires a mental inversion: *the point of liquidity is not return; it is control.*

This approach is also deeply embedded in the design of their financial architecture. Wealthy families do not simply hold cash; they create structures that replicate the effects of liquidity without bearing its full opportunity cost. For instance, they may hold units in short-duration credit funds, own dividend-paying businesses with flexible distributions, or establish revolving private credit vehicles that allow capital to be recalled as needed. These structures are not about convenience—they are about *resilience engineering.*

The concept of *optionality* is also vital here. Liquidity creates optionality—the ability to say "no," to wait, to decline suboptimal terms. It empowers strategic inaction, which in turn enables better long-term decisions. In this light, liquidity functions not just as a financial resource but as a behavioural hedge. Those who are forced to act—by circumstance, margin calls, or investor expectations—are more likely to lock in suboptimal outcomes. *The wealthy do not just buy assets; they buy time. Liquidity is how they do it.*

A key philosophical difference underpins this entire strategy: the enduring rich do not confuse activity with progress. In financial culture, particularly in times of exuberance, there is immense pressure to "put money to work." Cash is seen as idle, unproductive, or even cowardly. But among long-enduring dynasties, cash is not idle—it is *strategically latent.* It is capital that has not yet been asked to perform. And that decision—to wait, to hold, to retain optionality—is not a lack of conviction. It is *discipline masquerading as passivity.*

This principle is reinforced across generations. Wealthy families train heirs to value liquidity not as an emotional comfort, but as a strategic lever. Liquidity is integrated into trust mandates, family office operations, and governance protocols. Some even maintain *liquidity stress tests*, simulating scenarios in which capital must be accessed, moved, or preserved under adverse conditions. This is not reactive finance—it is *defensive foresight.*

Contrast this with many high-income professionals whose net worth may appear impressive but is locked into illiquid forms—founder equity, retirement accounts, restricted shares, or overleveraged real estate. Their financial posture may be impressive on a spreadsheet but brittle in real life. When the economy turns, their ability to exit, reposition, or preserve evaporates. Their "wealth" is contingent—*conditional upon circumstances they do not control.*

Moreover, liquidity also acts as a signalling device within elite financial networks. Those who can deploy capital without hesitation are treated differently—not merely as buyers or investors, but as *stabilisers* of systems. Liquidity conveys seriousness. It allows for private deal access, inside pricing, and trust-based negotiations. In this context, *liquidity is not just protective; it is relational.*

Finally, liquidity is a psychological advantage. Those who hold it are less anxious, less reactive, and more selective. They are less likely to over-commit, overpay, or over-leverage. This restraint, over time, compounds. The discipline of liquidity is not just financial—it is cognitive. It rewires one's relationship to urgency, risk, and reward.

The illusion that net worth equals strength has cost countless fortunes. Paper valuations rise and fall with markets. Liquidity, by contrast, remains a quiet constant—the unglamorous buffer that separates those who endure from those who fade. To stay rich is not to accumulate static assets but to maintain strategic flow. And in that flow lies the true measure of wealth: not what one has, but what one can *move*—and when.

Dry Powder: The Strategy of Waiting

The wealthiest individuals in the world are not merely distinguished by the size of their portfolios or the glamour of their assets. They are separated by their timing—more precisely, by their *capacity to wait.* This is not the romantic patience praised in proverbs; it is strategic, operationalised patience backed by liquidity. The rich stay rich not because they always act, but because they can afford not to. *Dry powder*—readily deployable cash held back during boom cycles—is not a sign of indecision or conservatism. It is a deliberate edge. And in environments where others are forced to liquidate, stall, or compromise, that edge becomes dominance.

Most people misread wealth as velocity. They look for movement—startups launched, properties acquired, trades executed—and assume motion signals financial vitality. But the wealthy understand that movement without optionality is chaos. During moments of economic stress, financial systems do not reward the bold so much as the prepared. And being prepared does not mean guessing right; it means having room to manoeuvre when others do not. Liquidity is not merely a cushion—it is a lever. It amplifies advantage precisely when the environment becomes unfavourable for everyone else.

This concept becomes most stark during downturns. When capital markets freeze, banks tighten lending, and asset prices decline, the average investor's instincts often turn reactive: cut losses, conserve energy, reduce exposure. But the wealthy behave asymmetrically in such conditions. Because they are not overexposed and are not chasing marginal gains, they are positioned to *buy* when others *must sell.* Their dry powder becomes offensive capital in a defensive climate.

Consider the 2008 global financial crisis. While tens of millions lost retirement accounts, homes, or jobs, a select few—armed with dry powder—went shopping. Warren Buffett's capital infusion into Goldman Sachs was not an act of bravado. It was a premium-priced opportunity offered to a cash holder when no one else had cash. That pattern repeated across distressed real estate, private equity, and infrastructure: liquidity purchased leverage at steep discounts.

The logic is subtle but consistent. In flush times, those with high exposure reap the greatest gains. But in corrections, those without exposure but *with cash* acquire the future at a discount. Most people miss this because they view liquidity as idle capital—money not "working." But the wealthy are not seduced by that productivity myth. *Cash does work—it just works through timing, not activity.* A cash reserve is not passive. It is a silent bid, waiting to be triggered when conditions flip. The very discipline to wait, to hold a non-performing asset (cash) while others chase returns, requires mental fortitude—and access.

This strategy is unavailable to most precisely because it requires margin: both financial and psychological. The middle class often cannot afford to hold significant dry powder. When interest rates are high and living costs unrelenting, unused capital feels wasteful. And culturally, the pressure to show progress—especially in entrepreneurial and professional circles—makes holding cash feel like cowardice or failure. But the wealthy are under no such illusion. Their metrics are not quarter-to-quarter but generation-to-generation. They do not need to demonstrate momentum; they need to sustain dominance. In that paradigm, *the ability to wait is not weakness—it is wealth itself.*

Dry powder also aligns with a broader decision-making rhythm among the wealthy: they avoid forcing moves. A family office, for instance, may spend years in portfolio stasis—not because of inaction, but because it is waiting for the environment to distort in its favour. This is not laziness; it is architecture. Holding capital until the world over-corrects is a form of strategic patience that turns panic into premium access. And crucially, *this kind of patience is not passive—it is surveillance married to restraint.* These families and institutions are watching constantly; they are just not moving reflexively.

There is also a cultural transmission aspect to the dry powder philosophy. Among ultra-wealthy families, the value of unallocated resources is taught early. Children are not just warned against reckless spending; they are trained to see cash reserves as a strategic asset. In family councils and investment committees, the conversation is often not "What can we buy?" but "When will our patience be rewarded?" In this view, capital is not merely fuel for consumption—it is leverage for timing. The goal is not maximum return but maximum *optionality*. And optionality requires you to *not* spend, *not* chase, *not* deploy—until the world tilts.

The discipline of waiting has historical roots as well. During the 1997 Asian financial crisis, numerous Western firms acquired controlling stakes in distressed Southeast Asian companies for pennies on the dollar. They had no specific foresight—they simply had capital when others were liquidating. In moments like these, *timing beats forecasting*. Having dry powder turns you from observer to actor when markets dislocate. And because these windows are brief, those already liquid act decisively while others are still recalibrating.

Yet, the psychological readiness to wait is often harder to cultivate than the financial mechanics. The mass-market investment ethos promotes urgency—buy now, sell high, beat the market. Platforms and pundits encourage constant motion. But the rich are not seduced by movement; they respect silence, wait for signal, and *pounce only when others are paralysed*. The reward is not just margin—it is access. Many of the best deals during crises are invitation-only, off-market, or contingent upon immediate capital. If you have to raise money to participate, you're too late. The price of admission is having already waited.

The strategy of dry powder is not merely about capital preservation—it is about advantage acquisition. While the average investor seeks to ride out the storm, the wealthy exploit the chaos. Not because they are smarter, but because they have margin—of error, of capital, of psychology. That margin is earned through structural restraint. They avoid over-leveraging in bull markets so they can dominate in bear ones. It is an approach grounded not in optimism, but in *readiness*. And readiness, more than return, is what defines capital that endures.

This is the unspoken secret of dry powder: it is not idle—it is armed. Those who hold it are not indecisive—they are disciplined. And the patience to wait, the clarity to act when others cannot, and the liquidity to seize dislocation—that is what turns crisis into compounding. Not for the next quarter, but for the next generation.

Owning Less, Controlling More

In modern wealth strategy, control—not mere ownership—is the game's real objective. The wealthiest individuals and families do not always appear wealthy in the conventional sense. Their names are rarely on the deeds, titles, or shareholder registries of the most valuable assets they influence. What they possess instead is structural leverage: the ability to direct capital without being encumbered by its legal, taxable, or reputational burdens. The idea that "he who owns, controls" is outdated in elite financial architecture. Increasingly, it is *he who controls without owning* who is best positioned to remain agile, private, and resilient across market cycles.

This distinction between ownership and control is not merely philosophical—it is operational. Asset-light structures such as irrevocable trusts, family holding companies, shell corporations, and multi-tiered equity partnerships enable the ultra-wealthy to separate legal title from effective authority. These vehicles offer protection, flexibility, and insulation—allowing individuals to manoeuvre without the drag of visibility or direct liability. Far from being exotic or esoteric, these tools are the bread and butter of modern dynastic wealth, designed not only to preserve capital but to shield the decision-making locus from political, legal, and economic volatility.

Trusts exemplify this elegantly. An irrevocable trust, for instance, can be constructed so that the settlor (the one who establishes it) no longer technically owns the assets. Yet if structured correctly, they can continue to influence how the assets are managed or distributed through tailored provisions and the strategic appointment of trustees. This allows wealth to be insulated from lawsuits, creditors, estate taxes, or even the personal liabilities of future generations—without sacrificing long-term control. When challenged in court, well-drafted trust agreements often hold up precisely because they encode authority in governance mechanisms, not personal possession. The benefit is not just legal shielding but long-range planning flexibility.

Shell entities, particularly in international jurisdictions, serve a different function: disconnection and discretion. In many cases, the appearance of detachment is the goal. A luxury property in London may be owned by a British Virgin Islands company, which itself is held by a family foundation in Liechtenstein, whose board includes trusted legal and financial advisers but not the beneficiaries directly. What this obfuscation achieves is not evasion, but leverage. It deters opportunistic lawsuits, stabilises reputational risk, and allows capital to flow across borders with minimal friction. The visibility threshold becomes strategic, not incidental.

Equity partnerships, particularly in private equity or real estate syndications, further demonstrate how the wealthy opt to influence rather than own. A high-net-worth individual might invest via a limited partnership structure where they control the general partner or have side-letter arrangements that confer disproportionate rights—such as veto powers, priority returns, or early exit clauses. Their equity stake may appear modest, but their actual authority can be considerable. In volatile markets, this setup allows them to walk away first, renegotiate terms, or liquidate with protective buffers—privileges unavailable to ordinary investors with greater nominal exposure.

The philosophy behind these structures is about optionality. Optionality is the right, but not the obligation, to act. In finance, it translates into the ability to delay, redirect, or reverse decisions without incurring immediate cost. For the wealthy, maintaining optionality is worth more than squeezing out an incremental return. It buys time, legal distance, strategic cover, and emotional calm during periods of market turbulence or family transition. When holding structures are opaque, portable, and flexible, the consequences of economic missteps are less catastrophic—both in perception and in practice.

Critics often equate such arrangements with secrecy or manipulation. But that analysis misses the underlying strategy. The goal is not to hide, but to *decouple.* By disentangling identity from capital, the elite gain room to manoeuvre. They can take risks with controlled entities while leaving the core estate insulated. They can test markets via partnerships rather than direct exposure. They can relocate assets without triggering headline consequences. In short, *control without ownership* is a stabilising mechanism in a world where visibility itself has become a liability.

Consider the case of a well-known American media tycoon who, during a contentious divorce, revealed that virtually none of his holdings were in his name. The properties, businesses, aircraft, and even artwork were technically owned by trusts or corporate shells. Though heavily scrutinised, these structures were found to be fully legal—and highly effective. Because he never owned the assets directly, they were largely shielded from claims. The strategy had been decades in the making, but it operated on a principle that anyone can understand: don't tie power to vulnerability. By outsourcing title but retaining governance, he preserved control while minimising exposure.

A similar dynamic is visible in sovereign wealth planning. Large family offices managing multi-generational fortunes often set up segregated legal compartments—each with its own trustees, objectives, and reporting lines. One vehicle may be focused on yield-producing assets with conservative mandates; another may explore high-growth opportunities with venture-style tolerance for loss. Importantly, the key decision-makers remain the same, but their authority is exercised through indirect command chains. This modular approach ensures that no single event—whether legal, reputational, or market-driven—can compromise the entire estate.

From a regulatory perspective, asset-light structures can tread a fine line. Increasingly, tax authorities and anti-money laundering agencies are scrutinising them. The OECD's Common Reporting Standard, the U.S. Foreign Account Tax Compliance Act (FATCA), and global beneficial ownership transparency rules are tightening the net around offshore havens and nominee arrangements. Yet for those who operate transparently within legal boundaries, the value of these structures remains undiminished. What's evolving is not their utility, but their sophistication. Modern wealth architects design them with forensic compliance and future-proof governance—not just discretion.

The real innovation is psychological as much as legal. Traditional thinking views ownership as the pinnacle of economic success. The ultra-wealthy view it as a liability—something to be disaggregated, delegated, and protected. Their focus is not on showcasing assets but preserving *agency*. That means being able to direct outcomes without being pinned down by headline ownership. In volatile environments—be they financial, political, or cultural—this separation becomes a source of enduring advantage.

This ethos also explains why asset-light wealth rarely draws attention. It does not signal status through visible opulence. There are no sprawling estates titled to individuals, no luxury vehicles bought outright. The impression is one of restraint, even frugality. But beneath the surface lies an intricate lattice of control—engineered for silence, resilience, and continuity. The true art is in the architecture, not the exhibition.

For those outside these circles, the lesson is not necessarily to emulate every legal manoeuvre. Many of these tools are expensive, complex, and jurisdictionally constrained. But the underlying mindset is broadly transferable. It's the mindset of *leverage through structure*, not accumulation through exposure. It's the discipline of placing capital one layer removed from the self—so that flexibility, protection, and strategic calm are always retained.

Owning less is not an abdication of wealth. It is a masterclass in its preservation. And in a world that rewards adaptability over display, it may be the most valuable asset of all.

Case Study: How the Savviest Stayed Liquid in 2008

In the fog of financial crisis, cash becomes clairvoyant. When the 2008 collapse arrived, it did not announce itself with a siren or calendar invite—it arrived as a slow and then sudden erosion of confidence, collateral, and counterparties. The wealthiest individuals who emerged not only intact but strategically advantaged were not necessarily the boldest risk-takers or the highest net-worth actors. They were the ones who held back when others rushed in, who refused to be seduced by leverage, and who understood—often through institutional memory—that liquidity is not a side detail of wealth management but its lifeline.

One of the great myths about the ultra-wealthy is that their fortunes are impervious to storms. But the 2008 global financial crisis eviscerated numerous "paper empires" whose net worths were inflated by fragile leverage structures—particularly those tied to real estate, hedge funds, and opaque credit derivatives. What separated the survivors was not insider information or exceptional forecasting ability, but discipline: a conscious refusal to maximise yield at the expense of resilience.

Consider how a figure like Seth Klarman, the founder of Baupost Group, positioned his fund before the crisis. Famously known for holding unusually large cash reserves—even as peers pursued double-digit gains—Klarman's strategy was derided by some in the hedge fund world as conservative or inefficient. Yet when the downturn came, Baupost was not only unharmed—it was poised. With liquidity intact and firepower ready, the fund was able to buy distressed assets at valuations that would have been unthinkable just months prior. *Dry powder was not idle; it was tactical patience.*

Contrast that with the fate of overleveraged real estate developers who had previously been lauded for their aggressiveness. Many entered 2008 with grand projects backed by short-term loans, secured on inflated appraisals. When the lending markets froze and asset prices plummeted, these developers didn't just lose profits—they lost solvency. Their empires were built on assumptions of refinancing that evaporated overnight. The distinction wasn't intelligence or boldness, but the presence—or absence—of strategic liquidity.

Liquidity is often misunderstood as the boring cousin of wealth. It doesn't dazzle like a portfolio of high-growth startups or a private jet hangar. But in moments of systemic distress, liquidity is what allows one to buy—while others are forced to sell. It's what allows investors to *name their price* in a distressed auction. And it's what transforms a downturn from a threat into an opportunity.

Many family offices internalised this lesson long before 2008, having watched prior cycles of exuberance and collapse. Among dynastic wealth holders, there exists a strong aversion to overexposure—even to "sure things." Liquidity, in their view, isn't just about financial positioning; it's about *freedom of action.* One Rockefeller trustee reportedly remarked that liquidity is what enables discretion, agility, and privacy during moments when others are boxed in by public scrutiny, forced asset sales, or covenant breaches.

Perhaps one of the clearest examples is how certain private equity veterans navigated the crisis. While mega-buyout firms suffered from stalled deal pipelines and credit crunches, more conservative funds—those that kept their powder dry—were able to acquire stakes in distressed competitors at fractions of book value. These weren't emergency buys; they were premeditated responses, honed by experience and an awareness of cyclicality. They knew that every ten-year bull run carries a shadow, and they waited—not by accident, but by design.

This design included more than just keeping money in treasuries or cash equivalents. It meant structuring portfolios with liquidity tiers: liquid assets for tactical use, semi-liquid holdings for strategic adjustments, and illiquid assets ringfenced with conservative debt ratios. In other words, these families and institutions didn't just have liquidity—they had *hierarchies of deployability*, so that when windows opened, capital flowed immediately and purposefully.

Compare this with affluent professionals—those in the upper-middle class who may technically be "rich" but functionally illiquid. Many were overexposed to housing markets, loaded with mortgage debt, and holding large positions in employer stock. They could quote financial terms with fluency and might even have appeared well-prepared on paper. But when the crisis hit, they were forced into defensive positions, liquidating assets at losses or, worse, losing access to capital entirely. *Knowing the rules of money is not the same as being immune to fragility.*

The individuals and families who thrived were often the ones who embraced what seems, on the surface, like inefficiency: they held cash, avoided the most tempting deals, and moved slowly. But slowness, in a mania, is not passivity—it's composure. They knew that *waiting is not the absence of strategy; it is a strategy*, especially when the environment is dominated by short-termism and yield-chasing.

A particularly revealing post-crisis analysis came from a small number of multi-family offices who disclosed that their most successful clients were those who had made no major moves in the two years leading up to the crash. They had quietly rebalanced, trimmed speculative positions, and resisted the pressure to "keep up" with faster-growing peers. When the market cratered, they weren't stunned into paralysis—they were ready to act.

That readiness wasn't fuelled by a single forecast but by infrastructure. These investors had trusted advisors, legal flexibility through shell entities or LLCs, and capital parked in fast-moving vehicles. It was not a matter of luck or raw talent. It was systems design. They had stress-tested their wealth against various scenarios, from liquidity freezes to credit default cascades, and had built in escape valves. *They didn't merely survive the crisis—they were structurally positioned to thrive within it.*

And that, perhaps, is the most underappreciated lesson of 2008: leverage magnifies risk, but liquidity multiplies opportunity. While most of the market was forced to play defence, those with capital and composure stepped into offensive roles. They bought stakes in bruised banks, recapitalised undervalued businesses, and entered partnerships on favourable terms—all because they could act when others couldn't.

This inversion—where waiting becomes a form of power—is not intuitive to many who operate under a growth-at-all-costs paradigm. But for the most sophisticated wealth holders, especially those guided by intergenerational thinking, it is a deeply internalised principle. Patience, in this context, is not passive; it is potent. The ability to hold back while the world accelerates is what makes it possible to accelerate when the world stalls.

2008 didn't just reveal who had made bad bets. It revealed who had built antifragility into their wealth architecture. The savviest didn't just avoid collapse—they converted it into leverage. Not by guessing better, but by *waiting better.*

Chapter 4
Playing Defense, Quietly

Enduring wealth is rarely the product of brilliance; it is more often the result of deliberate restraint. When markets wobble, the instinct of seasoned families is frequently not to act at all. This is not indecision—it is disciplined stillness cultivated over decades, a recognition that hurried responses tend to amplify losses. In a culture obsessed with movement, the truly affluent often default to patience, letting the noise settle before repositioning capital, exiting holdings, or recalibrating exposure. While the majority scramble to "do something," the dynastic approach asks a subtler question: how to avoid doing the wrong thing.

This philosophy—defensive, methodical, largely invisible—underpins the preservation of fortune. Public narratives glorify acquisition: bold investments, headline-grabbing portfolios, high-profile deals. Yet rarely do they highlight the back-office choices that avert disaster: insurance clauses drafted years in advance, re-domiciling of holding companies to mitigate geopolitical risk, or exiting a region quietly before it turns volatile. What appears as fortune in the public eye is often the product of protection first, performance second.

During corrections, the wealthy are not simply better capitalised—they are differently conditioned. They do not chase charts or attempt to catch falling knives. Instead, they ask measured questions: which exposures remain unseen? Where is optionality eroding? Which sources of liquidity are thinning? Their advantage lies in resisting the pressure to react immediately. This ability to pause, not from uncertainty but from informed clarity, permits decisions of higher precision. Across generations, those who preserve wealth consistently resist the impulse to solve disorder with speed.

Yet defence extends beyond inaction; it begins with structural preparation long before turbulence arrives. Insurance offers a prime example. Among the ultra-wealthy, policies protect not only property or art but reputation, contractual obligations, event risk, litigation, and even potential kidnapping scenarios. At this level, insurance is less about indemnification than about control—ensuring shocks do not cascade into legal or reputational crises.

Sophisticated families often construct coverage as meticulously as investment portfolios: stacking exposures across specialised carriers, layering overlapping policies that create legal moats, and leveraging global advisory teams to optimise jurisdictional advantages. It is unglamorous, yet profoundly effective. While others react to headlines, these families quietly execute clauses devised for precisely these tail events. Safety, here, is proactive scaffolding rather than a reactive net.

The depth of strategy extends into how risk is carried. Diversification becomes an architectural imperative. Exposure is not merely spread across sectors, but across legal regimes, political climates, currencies, and income sources. Multi-domicile structures are not about secrecy; they are about resilience. A natural disaster, regulatory change, or litigation risk can be absorbed differently when wealth is scattered across independent legal and geographic frameworks.

Location, in this calculus, is leverage. A Singaporean trust may shield against familial disputes in the US; a Liechtenstein foundation may separate control from taxable ownership. Income streams are deliberately heterogeneous: royalties, licensing, passive equity, and multigenerational leasing are valued not for glamour but for durability. Each stream is evaluated not solely for yield, but for survivability under stress.

Preservation also demands knowing when to retreat. Strategic exits—often underappreciated—are vital. Some families have divested from promising ventures, prestigious assets, or even entire regions, not out of panic but in anticipation of trajectory. They recognise that compounding applies not only to returns but to exposure. When jurisdictions or assets show opacity, friction, or legal ambiguity, the elite fold early, preserving optionality rather than gambling on hindsight. Exits are disguised as routine reallocations, ensuring discretion. For them, walking away is asymmetric defence—it safeguards the most precious asset in turbulence: the freedom to choose.

The idea that defensive wealth is passive is a misconception. Public displays of success—launches, acquisitions, IPOs—mask the quiet scaffolding designed to survive shocks. A trust may not excite, but it is difficult to litigate through. Diversified holdings rarely make headlines, yet are hard to seize. An insurance policy that never pays may seem wasteful until the day it preserves an entire estate.

The architecture of enduring wealth is inherently anti-fragile. It anticipates loss, panic, and unexpected correlations. It does not deny volatility; it trains for it. Legal exits are rehearsed, operational redundancies simulated, and structural instruments treated as assets. Defence is not reactive; it is proactive. The moves made in calm determine survival in storms.

This chapter examines how the most disciplined among the wealthy institutionalise restraint. It explores the transformation of insurance into strategic leverage, the deliberate orchestration of optionality, and the quiet, early, and deliberate retreats that underpin the survival—and sometimes amplification—of wealth across generations.

The First Move Is Often to Do Less

Panic creates noise. Wealth, when preserved over generations, responds with silence. In market corrections—those periods when headlines scream, liquidity evaporates, and institutional memory vanishes—what the enduring wealthy do first is *less than expected.* They do not sell into chaos. They do not reshuffle portfolios under duress. They do not pivot into the latest hedge. Their instinct is restraint—not from passivity, but from a cultivated resistance to the illusion of urgency.

This instinct is often misread by outsiders who equate high net worth with hyperactivity—deal-making, repositioning, and trading their way through volatility. But those who last, those who pass capital intact across three, four, or five generations, are not animated by motion. They are animated by structure. *Their default during turbulence is governed by design, not improvisation.* And that design assumes, from the outset, that volatility will arrive. The moment of correction, therefore, is not one of surprise—but of activation.

Consider the framing of risk in most investor education. The typical retail investor learns that downturns require action: rebalancing, sector rotation, tax-loss harvesting, or even exiting to cash. Financial punditry reinforces this logic—tactical, responsive, constantly adjusting. The elite, by contrast, have built portfolios with the express goal of *avoiding panic-driven decisions*. When volatility strikes, their first call is rarely to a brokerage—it's to a family office chief investment officer, whose mandate is not to "do something," but to verify that the core protective scaffolding is intact.

The silence that follows is not complacency—it is the space made by *good architecture*. A portfolio that has already hedged for downside does not require a defensive pivot. A trust insulated from capital gains tax consequences is not scrambling to meet redemptions. A diversified operating company with uncorrelated revenue streams is not racing to cover payroll. And so, the wealthy do not move—not because they're better informed in the moment, but because they prepared before the moment arrived. *The move not made is a decision already embedded in the system.*

Restraint is often misinterpreted by those without access to such systems. A middle-income investor forced to sell during a correction may view a wealthy individual's inactivity as luxury, not wisdom. But the distinction lies in leverage—psychological and structural. Those managing generational wealth are not typically playing for quarterly performance or social affirmation. Their primary game is *longevity under pressure*. The capacity to stay still in financial crisis is not a function of wealth—it is a function of not being exposed to the kind of debt, liquidity, or reputational fragility that demands reaction. *Liquidity is not just a line item—it is behavioural freedom.*

In 2008, as banks collapsed and credit froze, many wealthy families *did not sell a thing*. Instead, they reviewed longstanding agreements with private lenders, evaluated off-market opportunities, and confirmed coverage with insurers. Their first move was not to liquidate—but to confirm control. Even among hedge funds, those that survived—Bridgewater, Baupost, Citadel—did so not by trading more aggressively but by maintaining excess capital, risk parity frameworks, and tight governance around when not to act. *Success was found not in predicting the crash, but in withstanding it without flinching.*

This restraint is taught, not inherited. Among the enduring wealthy, family governance documents often include stipulations on reaction thresholds—requiring multiple signatures for asset sales, triggering hold periods during macro volatility, or explicitly forbidding short-term allocation shifts during stress periods. These are not bureaucratic overreaches—they are *psychological guardrails* that prevent precisely the kind of capitulation that destroys capital.

In practice, this means action is not banned, but *deliberately slowed.* A family foundation might wait 90 days after a correction before reallocating. A family office CIO may be restricted to rebalancing only within predefined asset class bands. Decision rights might be split between generations to force multilateral consensus. These mechanisms extend the time horizon not just in theory, but in implementation. *They operationalise patience.* And in doing so, they protect against the two worst errors during crisis: liquidity panic and emotional contagion.

It's important to differentiate this form of restraint from indifference or inaction. The elite do act—but they act *later, smaller, and more conditionally.* They are far more likely to wait for second-order effects to surface—defaults, bankruptcies, distressed sellers—before deploying capital. Where others buy the dip, they buy the delay. Their action is surgical, not reactive. *And the absence of early motion is what makes that later action so effective.*

Even among private entrepreneurs, restraint is a tell. In 2020, when COVID disrupted everything from real estate to logistics, many family-owned firms delayed decisions rather than issue blanket layoffs or attempt hasty pivots. They assessed how competitors would behave, how regulatory aid would be administered, how consumers would settle. While corporates announced immediate restructurings, these founders often pulled back *just enough* to conserve flexibility. When conditions stabilised, they had dry powder, loyal teams, and a less damaged brand. *The delay was not passive—it was an investment in optionality.*

Philosophically, this reflects a deeper worldview: that markets, like ecosystems, self-correct not through constant tinkering but through *systemic adaptation over time.* The enduring wealthy do not see volatility as a puzzle to be solved, but as a wave to be survived. Their strategies are built on *nonlinearity*, *uncertainty*, and *the irrelevance of certainty in the short term.* Their portfolios contain asymmetric exposure to upside, while their downside is insulated by structure, not just strategy.

For those managing or building wealth, the lesson is not simply "do less." It is to *build the kind of financial architecture that makes doing less a legitimate option.* That means structuring liquidity so it's not forced, establishing governance that slows fear, and defining success as preservation first. It means embracing the idea that the most intelligent move in crisis is often the *decision not made in haste.*

This subchapter does not glorify inactivity—it reframes it. It shows how *restraint is a form of power*, discipline a form of leverage, and inaction—when grounded in preparation—a form of radical intelligence. The first move is often to do less, because the cost of being wrong in motion is far greater than the cost of being right too late. The enduring wealthy know this—not because they fear risk, but because they've studied its rhythm across time. And time, not impulse, is the asset they defend most fiercely.

Insurance as a Sophisticated Game

Among the enduringly wealthy, insurance is not a postscript to planning—it is strategy in motion. Far from being a bureaucratic obligation or simple contingency plan, it is deployed as a surgical instrument to stabilise value, shift liability, and protect intangible assets in ways that elude conventional financial literacy. For the affluent, insurance is not just about mitigating risk; it is about buying strategic silence, legal shield, operational continuity, and, at times, reputational redemption. This reframing of insurance as a tactical lever—rather than a last resort—reveals a sophisticated game most never realise is being played.

The average individual sees insurance as a binary: you pay premiums in hopes of never needing them. The wealthy, by contrast, treat insurance as a fluid capital allocation tool—one that works in tandem with trusts, offshore vehicles, and legal arbitrage to create a reinforced architecture of protection. From rare art to litigation coverage, from key person policies to event cancellation clauses at high-profile galas, insurance serves to lock in certainty where others face exposure. This is not merely about preventing loss; it is about controlling narrative, shielding brand equity, and extending optionality.

Consider the role of insurance in the art world—a sector riddled with volatility, theft risk, and authenticity disputes. For ultra-high-net-worth collectors, fine art insurance is not simply a defensive hedge against fire or burglary. It's a prerequisite for mobility, enabling pieces to travel across borders, be shown at exhibitions, or stored in climate-controlled vaults under complex ownership arrangements. Insurers and underwriters become part of the logistics team, managing valuation fluctuations, legal jurisdictions, and diplomatic protocols. This kind of cover becomes an enabling force—not a barrier—empowering asset liquidity and geopolitical manoeuvring.

Litigation insurance is another arena where wealth deploys foresight few anticipate. Where most brace for court battles as devastating and unpredictable, the strategic elite engage litigation finance firms and carry policies that cover defence costs or payout liabilities for reputationally sensitive disputes. In some cases, this includes insuring against potential lawsuits from former employees, disgruntled partners, or regulatory overreach. The result: a capacity to engage in high-risk negotiation or enforcement without fearing ruinous consequences. It is not uncommon for these policies to be written in bespoke terms, negotiated directly between insurers, legal teams, and the family office—off-market, off-record, and off-limits to conventional structures.

Event insurance, particularly in the post-pandemic era, has transformed from a formality to a front-line instrument of reputation management. When a billionaire family hosts a philanthropic summit, wedding, or art auction, they insure not just the venue and logistics, but sometimes even the weather, the appearance of specific guests, or the non-occurrence of public scandal. These contracts are engineered to protect brand narratives as much as financial stakes. Cancellation due to reputational events—think lawsuits or negative press tied to key participants—can trigger recoveries. Thus, insurance becomes not just a buffer against mishaps, but a narrative governor.

Then there is reputation insurance itself—still a niche, lightly regulated terrain, but one growing in sophistication. This market, historically the domain of large corporations, is now being adapted to individuals with significant public exposure. Policies may cover crisis PR costs, cyber defamation campaigns, or even social media fallout from controversial family events. It is risk transfer, not just of capital, but of narrative volatility. For heirs with political ambitions or corporate portfolios, this protection can be more valuable than any real estate holding.

Bespoke insurance portfolios are increasingly curated not by brokers, but by multi-family offices and legal strategists. These portfolios often mirror the family's operating style, with policies written across jurisdictions to exploit regulatory asymmetries and maximise payout flexibility. For example, a UK-based trust may hold artworks insured through Luxembourg, litigated in Delaware, and physically stored in Geneva. Each decision is deliberate—not just about premium cost but about *jurisdictional insulation* and *capital control.*

What's essential to grasp here is not the individual policies but the philosophy that animates them: *insurability is leverage.* To be able to assign value to a potential risk and transfer that risk in exchange for liquidity—or credibility—grants the wealthy an asymmetric advantage in volatile environments. The ordinary investor reacts to chaos; the prepared elite *write policies into the chaos itself,* monetising volatility while protecting downside.

This is where contrast becomes sharp. Middle-class financial education teaches budgeting, asset allocation, and emergency savings. But for dynastic wealth, financial control emerges from mastering the interplay between tangible value and legal abstraction—knowing when to *own risk*, when to *transfer it*, and when to *mask it.* Insurance operates as the hidden language in this symphony. Where others hope to survive surprise, the strategic wealthy price it in—and often profit from it.

It would be reductive to frame these mechanisms as merely conservative or defensive. In many cases, insurance allows the wealthy to act with greater aggression. For instance, a hedge fund founder entering a politically sensitive market might take out reputational risk insurance in tandem with local litigation policies. This doesn't reflect fear—it reflects precision. The cover acts as a form of collateralised confidence, empowering faster, more decisive moves with a known floor.

This also extends to internal family dynamics. In cases where succession, inheritance, or divorce pose potential future destabilisers, key person or intra-family buyout insurance may be established. These policies provide liquidity on death or exit—preventing the fire-sale of assets or boardroom conflict. Thus, insurance becomes not only financial arbitration, but *relational governance.*

Notably, insurers have become more selective post-2008 and 2020, narrowing coverage, requiring increased disclosure, and placing pressure on transparency. But this, paradoxically, has only increased the premium on bespoke structuring. For the ultra-wealthy, policies now come embedded in broader governance models—linked to family constitutions, philanthropic mandates, and sovereign risk hedging. What emerges is not a market of policies, but of *financial architecture.* Insurance ceases to be the last line of defence. It becomes the first sketch of the fortress.

At its core, the strategic use of insurance among the wealthy reflects a profound truth about how power operates. It is not that they have fewer risks—it is that they get to price their risks, and by extension, *shape the context in which those risks occur.* While others brace against storms, they underwrite them. They are not simply buying protection. They are buying *optionality, continuity, and control.* That is what makes the game so sophisticated—and so invisible.

Geo, Asset, and Income Diversification

In environments defined by volatility—whether political, economic, or environmental—the capacity to disperse exposure is not simply a feature of wealth but a signature of its permanence. While most public discourse around diversification still hovers around portfolio theory and asset class allocation, dynastic wealth thinkers treat diversification not as a passive spread of investments, but as a multi-dimensional architecture of insulation. *To diversify, in their playbook, is to decentralise vulnerability itself—across jurisdictions, legal structures, asset classes, and revenue streams.* This structural complexity is not just a product of sophistication; it is a strategic necessity that underwrites endurance.

The financial elite do not merely hedge bets in equity markets. They hedge geography. It's not uncommon for families of enduring wealth to maintain homes across continents—not for leisure, but for legal and strategic optionality. Real estate in New York offers legal anchorage to U.S. tax codes, but residency in Switzerland or Singapore offers operational detachment in times of litigation, surveillance, or geopolitical instability. In many ultra-high-net-worth (UHNW) families, one generation might reside in London for access to European financial services, another in Dubai for tax leniency, and a third in Canada for educational and healthcare advantages. *Geographic diversification here is not cosmopolitanism—it's contingency planning.*

Legal diversification follows a similar logic. Holding structures are designed not simply to optimise tax but to firewall exposure. An individual may own nothing directly yet control vast sums through trusts, foundations, or special-purpose vehicles that hold assets across different regulatory domains. Consider a family that parks art collections in Luxembourg, operating companies in Delaware, and charitable arms in Liechtenstein—each serves not only a legal purpose but represents a different pressure valve under stress. *To diversify legally is to create layered sovereignty: if one jurisdiction falters, others remain operable.*

Operational diversification is perhaps the least discussed yet most telling aspect of the sophisticated defence strategies the wealthy employ. Multiple income streams—across real estate, private equity, passive licensing, royalties, and long-horizon investment vehicles—ensure that a shock to one sector does not disable the household's broader financial machinery. A billionaire who derives 60% of their income from legacy shipping routes will often own an early-stage fund in a technology vertical unrelated to transportation. Even within companies, shareholdings may be structured to limit dependency: minority equity positions across several boards yield less operational risk than a controlling stake in one vulnerable business. *To diversify income is to refuse monogamy to any one market's fate.*

What makes these layers of diversification so durable is their interlocking logic. A lawsuit in one country might be inconsequential if the majority of a family's assets are protected under a foreign trust. A crisis in one industry may be absorbed if income flows in from three others. A banking freeze in one jurisdiction is manageable if operating accounts exist across five continents. *Diversification, properly executed, is not about maximising upside—it is about limiting existential downside.*

This framework was not developed overnight. It is cultivated through cross-generational legal advisory, long-standing relationships with global banks, and embedded alliances with private wealth offices that specialise in risk-resilient structuring. In the Rockefeller family, for example, geographic and operational diversification wasn't a post-crisis fix but a guiding strategy from inception. Their trusts did not merely disburse capital—they required heirs to engage with investment committees, embedded fiduciaries, and global diversification mandates as part of their stewardship. These structures are not reactive but preventative.

Critically, this level of diversification demands a different cognitive model. The average investor may still see a diversified portfolio as owning a blend of stocks, bonds, and real estate. The enduringly wealthy conceptualise risk as cascading—capable of moving through reputational damage, regulatory clampdowns, or macroeconomic contagion. To survive such events, wealth must not only be multiplied—it must be fragmented, siloed, and internationally modular. *The model is not just about where capital is parked, but how fluidly it can move and how invisibly it can be protected.*

There are tensions, of course. Asset fragmentation can dilute focus. Operating across jurisdictions invites regulatory friction. Maintaining diversified legal entities requires constant legal and accounting oversight. But these costs are accepted as necessary overhead—the price of strategic agility. And increasingly, the ultra-wealthy understand that this agility is not merely defensive but generative. It allows capital to be moved toward opportunity with minimal friction. It permits families to respond to political shifts not with panic but with poise. It gives heirs optionality not only in investment but in residency, identity, and strategic withdrawal.

During the global financial crisis, families that had their fortunes concentrated in a single national banking system—such as Iceland or Cyprus—found themselves paralysed. Those who had structured their holdings across international jurisdictions not only weathered the storm but deployed capital at distressed discounts. Similarly, when political revolutions or sanctions struck parts of the Middle East, those with operational bases elsewhere sustained their enterprise value and personal mobility. *Geographic diversification isn't exotic—it's existential.*

This brings us to an uncomfortable yet necessary insight: true diversification is not accessible to everyone. Many strategies that the ultra-wealthy use to diversify legally or geographically require thresholds of capital, networks of advisors, and temporal patience that exceed the reach of most professionals. There is an inherent structural privilege in the ability to be hyper-mobile, hyper-informed, and hyper-advised. But to ignore the architecture of that privilege is to remain naïve to how sophisticated capital truly behaves under pressure. *Learning from these systems, even at a scaled-down level, offers ordinary investors a more realistic playbook for long-term security.*

That's why the study of elite diversification is less about emulation and more about mindset. It challenges the narrow fixation on returns and invites a broader inquiry into survivability. It redefines "security" not as insulation from volatility but as intelligent decentralisation of exposure. And it forces a deeper question—*not just how much one owns, but how resilient that ownership really is.* For those with wealth to preserve, that distinction is not academic. It is everything.

Strategic Retreats: Knowing When to Fold

The world's wealthiest are often assumed to possess an uncanny ability to take bold risks and emerge stronger. But this mythology of aggressive wealth-building obscures a quieter, subtler truth: *the enduring rich are often defined less by what they pursue, and more by what they abandon.* Strategic retreat—exiting early, refusing to double down, or walking away entirely—is not a failure of nerve. It is a form of elite discipline, honed over generations, that prioritises optionality and capital preservation above bravado.

When markets become unstable, the instinct of the unseasoned is action—more trades, rapid reallocations, hedges layered on hedges. Yet among enduring dynastic wealth, the first move is often subtraction. The ability to *cut exposure cleanly*, to exit without emotional attachment, is itself a form of advantage. It is the difference between playing for permanence and gambling for upside.

This restraint is not passive. It is strategic, premeditated, and often deeply contrarian. Many of the wealthiest families maintain internal 'red lines'—defined loss thresholds, sector-specific limits, or even moral filters—that trigger divestment regardless of what the broader market is doing. When institutional investors were still rationalising their positions in commercial real estate in 2006–2007, certain private family offices were already unloading exposures entirely—not because they had proof of collapse, but because *they had nothing to prove.* Their wealth was not on the line to validate a thesis.

That mindset—of *wealth as something to protect rather than prove*—is a foundational difference between newcomers and legacy capital. The latter understand that asymmetric survival matters more than asymmetric return. One high-magnitude loss can undo years of compounding. As such, strategic retreat is embedded into their governance frameworks: through liquidity buffers, voting rights that allow unilateral withdrawal, and exit clauses built into joint ventures from day one.

Consider the case of a major Latin American industrialist whose holding company quietly exited an entire tranche of infrastructure projects in Eastern Europe two years before regional conflict made headlines. To outsiders, the move appeared overly cautious—perhaps even capricious. But within the family's internal strategy group, the logic was precise: *thin rule-of-law environments coupled with currency instability had breached pre-set tolerances.* The decision, while early, avoided hundreds of millions in downstream impairment.

Contrast this with over-leveraged developers and PE firms in the same space, many of whom waited too long, misread the geopolitical signals, and found themselves entangled in capital controls or asset seizures. In the post-mortem of any financial crisis, the wealth that survives is almost always the capital that *left early, not cleverly.*

This contrarian rhythm—pulling out just as others lean in—requires more than information. It requires internal permission structures that reward quiet exits over loud victories. Many family offices and ultra-high-net-worth entities institutionalise this through bespoke investment committees comprised not of optimisers, but of sceptics—individuals tasked with asking what could go wrong, not how to stretch the upside. The power to veto, to stand still, or to shrink a position entirely is hardwired into their models.

There is also a critical legal and structural element to retreat-readiness. Wealth that cannot be exited is not real power. The most structurally sophisticated investors pre-load exit pathways into how they hold assets in the first place. Offshore trusts with liquidation provisions, nominee ownerships that allow discreet sale, convertible instruments with ratchet clauses—*these are not just tools of tax optimisation, but of exit readiness.* They enable liquidity without distress, and retreat without fanfare.

Silicon Valley offers an instructive contrast. During the dot-com bust of 2000–2001, many founders, flush with valuation-rich equity, were structurally trapped. Their wealth existed primarily in illiquid stock, with few mechanisms to exit without tanking the price. By comparison, several family-backed tech investors had already cashed out—through dual-class structures, secondary sales, or private equity recapitalisations. Their portfolios shrank in headline terms, but not in functional firepower.

The lesson is not that the rich know the future. They do not. But *they build portfolios with escape hatches.* That mindset reframes the entire philosophy of wealth: it is not a game of control, but of resilience. To fold—quietly, early, and without emotional residue—is often a privilege reserved for those who designed their capital to be light, agile, and unentangled.

Strategic retreat also extends beyond markets. It is present in the social and political positioning of dynastic wealth. During periods of regime instability, the savviest relocate jurisdictional exposure—not just assets, but heirs, legal residencies, and philanthropic headquarters. In certain Gulf states, for instance, several long-established European families maintain formal tax domicile but shift their children's schooling, family councils, or trustee operations to Switzerland or Singapore when local sentiment changes. This is not flight. It is *preservation by dispersion.*

Even in reputational terms, retreat has become a subtle art form. Wealth advisors now routinely recommend preemptive disclosures, quiet settlements, or the controlled unwinding of public ventures as a means of brand survival. Strategic silence, structured exits from board positions, or the withdrawal of family names from high-risk ventures are not acts of fear—they are signals of *meta-capital awareness.* The wealthy increasingly understand that brand equity, legal insulation, and narrative control are as fragile as asset prices. To protect them requires tactical withdrawal as much as strategic deployment.

What underlies all this is a deeper philosophical divergence: *most people conflate movement with progress.* But generational wealth sees endurance not as the ability to hold, but as the wisdom to let go. To them, liquidity is not just financial—*it is psychological.* The ability to walk away—to abandon what once worked, to shed unproductive complexity, or to preempt public fallout—demands a form of clarity that cannot be taught through standard financial literacy. It is a mindset conditioned by experience, structurally enabled by design, and reinforced by a deep understanding of fragility.

The great paradox is that retreat is invisible. No one celebrates a crisis avoided. No headlines are written about the fund that sold six months early. No statues are built for restraint. And yet, these are the moves that keep dynasties intact. The move that was never made. The deal that was never signed. The exposure that was trimmed. *That is where the real power resides.*

To the outside world, these manoeuvres look like luck, or cowardice, or insider access. But to those who understand the inner logic of capital, strategic retreat is not a sign of fear—it is the highest expression of confidence. The confidence to do less. To disappear from danger. To win by vanishing before the storm hits.

Chapter 5
Hidden in Plain Sight

If you happened upon a casual dinner among self-made millionaires, you might overhear talk of equity rounds, crypto speculation, aviation leases, or cutting-edge technology ventures. Step into a closed-room gathering of enduring family wealth—trustees of century-old foundations, delegates of sovereign funds, or family office principals—and the conversation shifts to a far quieter register: regulated utilities, timberland, triple-net leases, subordinated private debt. Enduring capital rarely seeks the spotlight; it grows in the shadows.

The widespread fantasy among aspirational investors is that wealth springs from dazzling foresight, audacious bets, or impeccable timing. Occasionally, this is true. But those who preserve fortune across generations more often rely on assets that appear, at first glance, almost dull. Slow-yielding, uncorrelated, operationally mundane investments—no ticker symbols, no viral stories, no retail frenzy—dominate the portfolios of those with everything to lose.

Consider farmland, municipal bonds, or catastrophe reinsurance: these seldom feature in mainstream finance media. Their complexity, opacity, or illiquidity renders them unsuitable for mass consumption. Yet precisely because they evade attention, they attract less volatility, fewer amateurs, and far less noise. The yield they offer is structurally managed, not subject to the whims of sentiment or short-term momentum.

Understanding this divide—between the headline-grabbing assets and quietly compounding holdings—is crucial to grasping elite investment logic. It's not only what the wealthy acquire, but what they deliberately avoid discussing. Their most valuable instruments are often invisible to the public eye, not for secrecy alone, but because the market structures around them defy conventional exposure. Farmland aggregators, litigation finance, specialised leasing trusts, carbon credit markets, and direct lending platforms are challenging to explain at cocktail parties, yet they underpin much of long-lived wealth.

Take private credit, for instance. While the public crowds into bond markets, elite capital quietly underwrites middle-market loans to businesses excluded from traditional financing. Collateral, governance rights, and equity participation grant control and downside protection. These deals require rigorous due diligence and patient capital. They rarely make headlines but provide something conventional instruments cannot: pricing power and structural safety.

Or consider farmland. To the casual observer, land lacks the glamour of tech IPOs or commercial towers. Yet for families with a centennial horizon, productive land delivers inflation hedges, layered cash flows—from crops to water rights—and estate planning advantages, all while remaining largely uncorrelated with public markets. During the 2008 downturn, some North American farming collectives expanded acreage even as equity markets collapsed. Not flashy, but ballast.

This taste for the unglamorous is not elitist affectation; it reflects asymmetric access and information. The most attractive, lowest-volatility investments rarely exist on public exchanges. They move through off-market syndicates, private networks, or bespoke mandates. The wealthy pay for performance, yes—but also for discretion. Off-market assets are not alternatives—they are a parallel financial universe, governed by distinct timelines, incentives, and gatekeepers.

Perhaps counterintuitively, the wealthy often embrace illiquidity. Long lock-ups in private funds, staggered vehicles, and bespoke trusts are designed intentionally: a form of self-discipline. By pre-committing to structures that cannot be disturbed impulsively, they mitigate the temptation to overreact, chase noise, or rebalance emotionally. Liquidity, here, is not always a virtue—it is a temptation to be resisted.

These strategies—private credit, off-market real estate, infrastructure concessions, litigation finance, insurance-linked securities—do not appear in undergraduate textbooks. They are transmitted through networks, whispered over dinners, or accessed via boutique intermediaries. To outsiders, this system can feel arcane or exclusionary. Yet it is not secrecy per se that creates value; it is structural discipline, information asymmetry, and horizon arbitrage.

None of this implies these assets are without risk. Many are operationally complex, demanding expertise to underwrite. What distinguishes them is that their risks are knowable, negotiable, and controllable—contrasting with public markets, where exposure is often externally dictated. In this parallel ecosystem, capital is actively shaped rather than passively allocated.

Conceptually, this reveals a profound truth: enduring wealth prizes stability over peak yield. The goal is not to chase the highest returns but to reduce the probability of unpleasant surprises. The elite seek clean lines from deployment to value realisation, insulated from crowd psychology and platform friction. They prioritise control over spectacle.

To grasp how dynastic fortunes persist, one must look beyond stock tickers, fund rankings, and social chatter. The signal lies in the deliberate silences: where others see dullness, the wealthy see durability; where others see complexity, they see defensibility; where others demand liquidity, they engineer lock-in. The ultimate game is not to appear clever today, but to remain solvent decades hence.

This chapter unveils those quietly potent instruments and strategies that never grace headlines but reliably preserve and grow wealth. It is not a checklist of investments, but a lens to understand how the most at-risk capital is safeguarded—not to triumph in a single quarter, but to endure across a century. Welcome to the hidden architecture of lasting wealth.

The Value of Boring Investments

It is an enduring irony of serious wealth: while public fascination with money gravitates toward stories of risky startups, aggressive trading, and speculative triumphs, much of the real capital that endures across generations is quietly parked in assets that most financial media barely find worth discussing. The wealthy, especially those who stay wealthy, have long demonstrated a counterintuitive truth: *boring investments are often the most powerful.* These are the slow-moving, cash-generating, volatility-resistant vehicles that rarely make headlines but consistently do their job—preserve capital, compound returns, and buy time during storms.

This is not a new phenomenon. In fact, one of the most misunderstood patterns among durable capital holders is their overwhelming preference for yield over glamour. They do not chase financial fireworks—they build cash flow engines. Think farmland instead of fast growth, multi-family rentals over meme stocks, insurance-linked securities instead of frontier crypto tokens. The logic is unromantic, yet deeply strategic: wealth is not only about what you earn, but about what you can reliably keep earning—quarter after quarter, regardless of sentiment or cycles.

To understand this philosophy, we must first disabuse ourselves of a myth hardwired into public thinking: that high returns must be dramatic to be meaningful. The enduring wealthy take a different view. They are less interested in doubling money in a year and more focused on assets that yield 6–10% reliably, year after year, in ways that don't keep them up at night. *They pursue peace of mind over performance theatre.* And because their capital base is large, even modest returns become meaningful at scale.

Consider timberland—one of the least-discussed assets in the public imagination, yet a darling of family offices, legacy funds, and generational portfolios. Timber grows regardless of who is in office or where interest rates sit. It has intrinsic biological yield. It provides inflation hedging and low correlation with equities. And perhaps most importantly, it has use-case universality—wood is unlikely to fall out of favour. The financial media may not celebrate this space, but the ultra-wealthy quietly accumulate it. *It's not just yield—it's insulation.*

The same pattern holds with farmland. It is arguably the most ancient form of real asset, and yet its relevance has never declined. Unlike tech equity or even gold, farmland produces something inherently needed: food. Over the last few decades, wealthy families and sovereign funds alike have increased their allocation to agricultural land—not for its speculative potential, but for its stability, scarcity, and productivity. An acre of irrigated cropland might yield a modest 3–6% annual return, but it also serves as a hedge against inflation, geopolitical instability, and fiat depreciation. It's tangible, self-sustaining, and globally strategic.

Why are these assets overlooked by the general investing public? Because they are not easily accessed, advertised, or understood. Platforms don't promote them. Influencers don't pitch them. Retail investors, driven by social momentum and digital dopamine, tend to overlook investments that lack visual excitement. *Boring doesn't trend.* But among the wealthy, that's precisely the appeal. Boring means predictable. Predictable means model-able. And model-able means you can plan—not just for a quarter, but for a decade.

One might argue that such instruments only become viable once a certain wealth threshold is passed. And to a degree, this is true: farmland, timber, and private credit are not always fractionalised or liquid. But the real takeaway is behavioural, not financial. The wealthy have a deep appreciation for cash flow predictability, capital durability, and structure over speculation. They are willing to trade upside fantasy for downside insulation. They know that compounding works best when left undisturbed, and *that the real enemy of wealth is volatility paired with illiquidity at the wrong moment.*

Take private credit. Often inaccessible to small investors, it nonetheless plays an outsized role in high-net-worth portfolios. Rather than lending via bond markets or public banks, the wealthy often act as private lenders—financing mid-sized enterprises, property developments, or secured receivables. The returns can range from 8% to 15%, backed by collateral and covenants. The model isn't new. What's new is how systematically it has replaced public bond exposure among family offices and endowments. The reason? Greater control, higher yield, and less mark-to-market volatility.

Another quiet bastion of boring yield is insurance-linked securities (ILS)—vehicles that tie returns to non-financial risks like natural disasters. Investors assume risks normally underwritten by insurers—catastrophe bonds, reinsurance contracts—and are compensated with premiums uncorrelated with the broader economy. While this space requires domain expertise, its philosophical appeal is clear: it adds orthogonal return streams to portfolios built for resilience, not just growth. Once again, *the wealthy aren't looking for bets—they're seeking ballast.*

This preference also extends into lifestyle-aligned assets that produce steady cash flows: storage facilities, mobile home parks, and even RV parking franchises. They are not glamorous, but they tap durable demand. They don't scale like venture-backed startups, but they compound steadily and insulate owners from macroeconomic drama. The operating risks are often lower, the customer churn manageable, and the maintenance requirements minimal. *These assets are not sexy, but they are sovereign.*

Importantly, these investments serve not only as sources of income but also as strategic levers. When your base portfolio throws off reliable yield, it allows you to act decisively during dislocations. Boring investments create flexibility. They reduce pressure to liquidate high-conviction positions or chase volatile opportunities just to meet expenses. *In a downturn, yield is defence. In a recovery, it becomes dry powder.*

Contrast this with portfolios skewed toward illiquid, high-beta assets with no current income. Their value may rise in boom years, but during contractions, they often drop fastest and can't be monetised. This creates stress, forced selling, or expensive borrowing—all of which destroy compounding. The lesson is subtle but profound: *yield protects the foundation; appreciation is the bonus.* The truly sophisticated investor does not reverse that equation.

What does this mean for the aspirational investor or emerging wealth builder? It's not that everyone must acquire timber or underwrite reinsurance. It's that *the mindset matters.* Focus on durability. Embrace predictability. Seek cash-generating positions that don't require perfect timing or constant oversight. And most critically, rethink the aesthetic of wealth. The flashiest portfolio isn't the strongest. Often, the strongest is the one you'd overlook if you didn't know better.

The wealthy understand that *boring is a feature, not a flaw.* Their portfolios don't try to impress—they try to survive, compound, and beget freedom. They are designed to be stable when others are panicking and opportunistic when others are frozen. In a world that glorifies risk-taking, it is the quiet engines—the farms, the bonds, the bridges, the loans—that actually keep dynasties intact.

What's hidden in plain sight is often ignored by the masses precisely because it looks unremarkable. But to the disciplined, the strategic, and the experienced, these so-called "boring" investments represent the height of sophistication: yield without drama, control without noise, and wealth without spectacle. That, more than any headline-making trade, is what real financial maturity looks like.

Why Some Assets Don't Get Talked About

In the modern theatre of personal finance, visibility is often mistaken for value. The investments that dominate headlines—tech IPOs, crypto booms, meme stocks, high-frequency trades—are not necessarily the ones held by families that have preserved wealth across generations. What the mainstream glorifies as bold innovation, many of the quietly enduring rich view as noise. Their portfolios often tell a different story—one of farmland in Iowa, private credit funds in Luxembourg, and catastrophe bonds tied to weather events in the Caribbean. These are assets rarely discussed at dinner parties or financial planning seminars. Yet they occupy a central place in the strategic playbooks of those who treat wealth not as a lottery win to be flaunted, but as an intergenerational trust to be quietly defended.

The reasons these assets remain under-discussed are not incidental—they are intrinsic to how real wealth is built and shielded. Unlike tech unicorns or speculative derivatives, they lack narrative glamour. They do not deliver "ten-bagger" returns in 18 months, nor do they feature in media stories that fetishise volatility as opportunity. What they offer instead is structural resilience, cash flow consistency, and a form of countercyclical utility that becomes apparent only when everything else falters.

Consider farmland. It produces income regardless of whether the NASDAQ is up or down. It has inherent biological productivity, inflation-linked pricing, and historically low correlation to equity markets. What's more, in many cases, it offers tax advantages through depreciation, conservation easements, and agricultural incentives. Yet farmland is almost never featured on retail investment platforms. Why? Because it's illiquid, operationally intensive, and difficult to securitise at scale. That makes it perfect for institutional investors, family offices, and high-net-worth individuals who care less about exit liquidity and more about asset permanence. It doesn't trade daily, and that's the point. Its value lies in its stability, not its visibility.

Private credit is similarly obscured, yet equally strategic. As banks stepped back from mid-market lending after the 2008 financial crisis—due to tighter capital regulations—private lenders stepped in. These non-bank institutions provide tailored financing to companies often too complex or niche for traditional underwriting. For wealthy investors, private credit offers fixed income-like cash flows but with higher yields and negotiated protections. Importantly, access to these deals is relationship-based. There is no app, no ETF, no gamified platform. The opacity is part of the value—it creates barriers to entry, which in turn sustains pricing power for those on the inside.

Insurance-linked securities (ILS) add another layer of defensive sophistication. These are instruments where investors assume insurance risk—like the occurrence of a hurricane or earthquake—in exchange for premiums. In essence, they allow non-insurers to enter the reinsurance market. What makes ILS remarkable is their detachment from traditional financial cycles. When markets plunge due to recession or geopolitical shocks, a windstorm in Florida or a typhoon in Japan is unmoved. For the structurally wealthy, this represents not just diversification, but orthogonality—a true decoupling from portfolio beta. And again, the public is rarely aware of this category. It lacks the human drama of equities or the tribalism of crypto. It operates in a different dimension—quiet, technical, effective.

There's also a sociological element at play. Many of these "unspoken" assets require not just capital, but context—legal, operational, and relational infrastructure that sits outside mainstream investing education. Farmland often comes through trust structures or legacy ownership networks. Private credit is gated behind limited partnership agreements and lengthy due diligence cycles. ILS is dominated by specialist reinsurers and Bermuda-based syndicates. These are not assets you can casually allocate to after watching a YouTube explainer. They are acquired through access, expertise, and a willingness to trade simplicity for asymmetry.

Mainstream finance, in contrast, sells clarity. It thrives on products that are easy to explain, easy to sell, and easy to liquidate. ETFs, index funds, and robo-advisors are tailored for this world. They are scalable, standardised, and liquid—precisely the traits that make them attractive to the masses and unattractive to long-term wealth architects. The latter know that what is scalable to millions is rarely durable over decades. In fact, the very mechanisms that make an investment "mainstreamable"—regulatory homogeneity, retail platform access, passive fund inclusion—often undermine its uniqueness as a store of value.

To be clear, none of this implies that farmland, private credit, or ILS are risk-free. Far from it. Each carries its own complexity and vulnerability. Farmland can be subject to climate risk, regulatory shifts, or commodity price swings. Private credit is exposed to credit defaults and illiquidity risk. ILS can suffer catastrophic losses in the event of tail-risk events. But what distinguishes these assets is how they interact with systemic risk. Unlike equities that nosedive in synchrony or bonds that suffer from rate shocks, these vehicles behave idiosyncratically. They wobble when others crash. And for sophisticated allocators, that behavioural asymmetry is worth more than a few extra percentage points of return.

There's also a tactical dimension to this obscurity. When an asset becomes widely talked about, it often becomes mispriced. The act of narrative proliferation—amplified by media, fund flows, and algorithmic trading—compresses its margin of safety. The wealthy understand this intuitively. They prefer assets that are hard to tweet about, because silence preserves edge. What doesn't get talked about doesn't get crowded. What doesn't get crowded doesn't get distorted. In a world where noise is monetised, silence becomes alpha.

Off-market investments are not a sign of elitism—they are a function of different constraints. Retail investors often need daily liquidity, platform accessibility, and regulatory clarity. The wealthy don't. They can pursue complexity if it offers convexity. They can accept opaqueness if it delivers control. They can tolerate illiquidity if it rewards patience. And so they allocate accordingly—not because they're hiding something, but because they're building something the public isn't trained to see.

The result is a portfolio that often looks "boring" from the outside but is quietly engineered for endurance. It throws off predictable income. It hedges across dimensions—economic, legal, and climatic. It doesn't need to outperform in every cycle because it survives across cycles. Its returns may be muted during bull markets, but they become dominant when volatility returns, liquidity dries up, and capital gets punished for being overexposed. That's when farmland looks genius, private credit looks prescient, and catastrophe bonds look prophetic.

Ultimately, the assets that don't get talked about are often the ones that don't need to shout. They just need to work. And for those who measure wealth in decades—not quarters—that is the only metric that matters.

Off-Market Advantage

The wealthiest individuals rarely buy at retail. That's not a statement about consumption—it's a principle of capital deployment. In public markets, information is priced instantly, sentiment is fickle, and reaction time is democratised. Everyone sees the same Bloomberg terminal. But real advantage—the kind that compounds power rather than merely money—lies not in reacting quicker, but in moving earlier. Long before a company IPOs, a property hits a listing service, or an asset class becomes investable through an ETF, private networks are already circulating ideas, term sheets, and off-market opportunities. What's hidden from the public eye is not necessarily obscure. It's reserved.

Off-market deal flow is the arterial system of quiet capital. It is the realm where access trumps speed, where trust replaces transparency, and where price is often a secondary concern to structure. It includes seed investments negotiated over private dinners, real estate portfolios traded through family office syndicates, and distressed assets transacted before courts or brokers get involved. These deals rarely rely on glossy pitch decks or cold outreach. They are invitation-only. And that exclusivity is not a form of elitism; it is a filtration mechanism. It weeds out volatility, litigation risk, and marketing-driven froth. *It is not just about getting a good deal—it's about controlling the variables around the deal itself.*

The average investor operates within public pricing ecosystems—stock exchanges, crowdfunding portals, or real estate platforms—because those ecosystems are designed to scale. They require disclosure, enforce symmetry, and encourage liquidity. But scalability often necessitates simplification. Terms are standardised. Due diligence is surface-level. And participation is passive. Off-market transactions, by contrast, demand deeper engagement. Investors shape the terms, design the capital stack, negotiate exit rights, and even co-manage the asset's operational arc. The price might not be lower—but the control is higher. And for serious capital, control is not a bonus; it is the primary hedge.

This is not simply about being early to trends. Timing matters, but it is only part of the advantage. More important is asymmetry—the ability to participate in upside without being fully exposed to downside. In public markets, that asymmetry is rare because pricing reflects consensus. Everyone plays the same game with similar rules. In off-market environments, terms are bespoke. Investors can negotiate liquidation preferences, ratchets, veto rights, or profit-sharing arrangements that fundamentally alter the payoff structure. A £10 million investment might yield mediocre returns in the public market if the timing is off. That same sum, invested off-market under protective covenants, could become a cornerstone holding—even if the company doesn't outperform benchmarks.

Private equity is perhaps the most institutionalised version of this model, but it is only one expression of a broader mindset. There is off-market everything: off-market debt, off-market art, off-market litigation finance, off-market insurance risk, even off-market philanthropy (through donor-advised funds or targeted impact deals). The defining feature is not the asset class—it is the structure of access. If you must apply for permission to invest, or if the deal is never advertised, it likely belongs to this world. And while regulation increasingly seeks to flatten the playing field, the nature of human trust networks makes true flattening impossible. Gatekeepers shift, but gates remain.

It's worth exploring why these deals stay hidden from the mainstream. In some cases, it is by design. Family-owned businesses looking for liquidity without exposure. Wealth holders offloading assets discreetly to avoid market slippage. Governments or institutions solving balance sheet issues through private placements rather than bond markets. But more often, the opacity is cultural. The most interesting deals are built on relationships, not roadshows. They circulate through alumni networks, intergenerational wealth channels, discreet intermediaries, and affinity groups with shared norms. These channels are opaque not because they are corrupt, but because they are personal. And trust, once earned, compounds into information advantage.

There is also an epistemic divide. Most financial media and education systems are not set up to teach how to access or interpret off-market opportunities. They teach how to read balance sheets, pick index funds, and avoid scams. Sensible skills for the general public—but insufficient for those managing generational wealth. Navigating off-market terrain requires a different skill set: relationship curation, legal nuance, tax sensitivity, and above all, patience. These deals are rarely fast. They require diligence not just of assets but of partners. And they demand readiness—because when a great off-market opportunity appears, there is little time to syndicate, deliberate, or hedge.

Critics of this model often point to opacity as a risk factor—and rightly so. Without public pricing, how do you know you're not overpaying? Without regulation, how do you protect against fraud? These are valid concerns. But they underestimate the internal governance standards of elite capital circles. The reputational stakes are higher in small networks. Word travels faster than lawsuits. And because many deals are serial—meaning investors expect to transact again with the same counterparties—there is built-in accountability. *In off-market environments, your name is your audit trail.*

The implications for wealth strategy are profound. First, access to off-market deals becomes a form of competitive insulation. You are no longer forced to chase yield in overcrowded markets. Second, it allows for thematic investing that doesn't rely on fund managers. You can back the future of agri-tech, space logistics, or regenerative medicine not by buying ETFs, but by owning pieces of companies, patents, or projects before Wall Street knows they exist. Third, it enhances privacy and discretion—values increasingly scarce in a digitised world.

But perhaps most important is the temporal reorientation. Public markets incentivise short-termism. Quarterly earnings, daily liquidity, real-time feedback loops. Off-market investing resets the clock. You are not rewarded for reacting—you are rewarded for being positioned. That posture favours those with long time horizons, disciplined underwriting, and social capital to navigate ambiguity. It shifts the measure of success from "How much did I make this month?" to "What systems did I strengthen for the next 20 years?"

This is not a model available to everyone. Nor should it be. Markets require layers—some liquid and transparent, others illiquid and opaque. The myth is that all opportunities should be equal. The reality is that opportunity, like knowledge, accrues where preparation meets context. Off-market advantage is not about privilege in the shallow sense—it is about positioning in the strategic sense. Those who cultivate the networks, skillsets, and capital structure to participate in this world are not merely richer in financial terms. They are *architects* rather than renters of their economic future.

In a world obsessed with market timing and trendspotting, the quiet power of off-market access reminds us that the best opportunities are not always priced—they are placed. And those placements go to those who are ready, not merely watching.

Illiquidity as Intentional Strategy

Liquidity is often mistaken for security. The prevailing logic, especially among retail investors and middle-market wealth holders, is that access equals safety. The ability to exit quickly is equated with control, as though freedom of movement inherently provides optionality. Yet among those managing serious, long-duration capital, the instinct often bends the other way: *true control lies not in the ability to flee, but in the willingness to stay.* Illiquidity, in these circles, is not an accident of structure or a drawback of esoteric investments—it is a feature, cultivated deliberately to enforce discipline, align incentives, and elongate the mental time horizon. To those trained in institutional-grade wealth management, *locking up capital is not a concession—it's a strategy of intent.*

This may seem counterintuitive in a world obsessed with agility. Financial media celebrates the ability to reposition portfolios in real time, hedge positions instantly, and chase alpha with surgical precision. Liquidity is heralded as the modern investor's superpower. But that view, though popular, is also deeply transactional. It assumes the investor is reactive—an opportunist trying to arbitrage volatility. Wealth holders who've endured across cycles tend to invert this frame. Their objective is not to out-trade others, but to *outlast them.* Liquidity, when always accessible, is a temptation to break one's own strategy. It invites second-guessing, encourages over-responsiveness to news flow, and enables emotionally driven portfolio churn.

Consider how the ultra-wealthy structure their core capital. Endowments like Yale's or sovereign wealth funds like Norway's do not allocate the majority of assets to publicly traded, daily-liquid securities. Instead, they allocate heavily to private equity, venture capital, infrastructure, and direct real assets—vehicles where capital is locked in for years, sometimes a decade or more. This isn't laziness or lack of access to liquid tools. It's a design choice. *Illiquidity acts as a firewall between conviction and emotion.* It enforces patience. It deters exit during moments of doubt. And perhaps most critically, it strengthens alignment between capital provider and capital user—because both are bound to the same long arc.

This commitment mechanism is especially relevant in environments of heightened noise. Financial panic, whether triggered by geopolitical events, pandemics, or algorithmic sell-offs, feeds on liquidity. The very ability to exit becomes the accelerant to instability. Investors who are "locked in" cannot participate in the stampede—not because they are more rational, but because they are structurally restrained. Ironically, this often yields superior long-term returns, not due to superior forecasting, but *because the constraint suppresses unforced errors.*

Illiquidity also serves a signalling function. Within the world of private capital, willingness to accept long lock-up terms is read as a badge of seriousness. Founders prefer cap tables populated by investors who won't demand quick exits. Fund managers seek limited partners who understand J-curves. Infrastructure projects and renewable energy developers look for financiers whose timeline matches the build-and-monetise cadence of their industry. In this sense, illiquidity is not just a risk—it is a credential. It signals alignment, patience, and partnership. The best deals, unsurprisingly, often require it.

The psychological benefits of illiquidity are less often discussed, but no less real. Behavioural finance has long shown that frequent observation of volatile assets leads to poorer decisions. The "myopic loss aversion" phenomenon—where investors disproportionately fear short-term losses despite long-term gains—is amplified when assets are marked-to-market constantly. Illiquid investments, precisely because they are not repriced daily, *shield the investor from their own nervous system.* The asset may fluctuate in underlying value, but without the trigger of a real-time quote, the impulse to intervene weakens. This promotes a healthier, more detached form of stewardship.

Critics argue, not without reason, that illiquidity can mask underperformance. Without regular price discovery, it's easy for underwhelming assets to hide inside private portfolios. This is a risk, and an important one. But it is not inherent to illiquidity—it is a function of governance. The most sophisticated investors address this through rigorous internal valuation protocols, independent audits, and detailed cash flow modelling. Transparency does not require liquidity; it requires oversight. And for those with the capacity to manage that oversight, *illiquidity unlocks access to returns that liquid markets often cannot offer.*

This asymmetry is particularly evident in niche or emerging assets. Take timberland, regenerative agriculture, or insurance-linked securities. These are not investments suited to daily trading—they require long holding periods, specialist knowledge, and patience for uncorrelated yield. Yet their return profiles, particularly after adjusting for volatility, rival and often exceed traditional asset classes. Similarly, venture capital—perhaps the ultimate illiquid asset—has historically delivered some of the strongest returns to early investors in transformative companies. But it requires surrendering not only control over the exit, but visibility over short-term valuation. Illiquidity is the price of access.

There is also a strategic dimension to locking up wealth. By removing capital from immediate use, it reduces the temptation for lifestyle inflation, distraction, or undisciplined diversification. Trust structures, private foundations, endowment models, and long-term limited partnerships all serve this purpose in different ways. They force the wealth holder to distinguish between *available capital* and *mission capital.* The former may serve near-term obligations; the latter becomes a vehicle for legacy, stewardship, or transformative investment. Illiquidity becomes a line in the sand—a structural commitment to future selves over present convenience.

It is no accident that many of the most enduring family offices and dynastic fortunes embrace forms of self-imposed illiquidity. They do not seek to trade their way to permanence; they architect permanence by baking it into the design. The wealth is not a pool; it is a dam. Not because they fear market collapse, but because they understand *continuity requires constraints.* A family that can liquidate everything in 48 hours may one day do so—whether in panic, conflict, or through generational misalignment. Capital that is constrained by structure rather than sentiment is less vulnerable to entropy.

There is, of course, a trade-off. Illiquidity introduces opportunity cost. It limits agility. It can create a mismatch between capital and liability timelines if not carefully managed. But these are solvable problems. Liquidity buffers, diversified income streams, and prudent leverage can address them. What matters is that the illiquidity is intentional—not accidental, not imposed, but *engineered* as part of a broader wealth philosophy.

The prevailing culture of financial immediacy will always underprice the value of stillness. But those who steward wealth at scale understand that *not everything valuable is visible, and not everything visible is valuable.* The freedom to act at will is seductive; the discipline to *not* act is protective. And in a world where noise increases, where reaction is the default, and where patience is increasingly rare, *illiquidity is not a burden—it is a moat.* It guards not just assets, but strategy. Not just returns, but intention. And for those who play the long game—not to win quarterly, but to endure generationally—it remains one of the most underappreciated forms of capital design.

Chapter 6
Social Capital Is Financial Capital

Durable wealth is rarely confined to portfolios, property, or even well-timed market plays. Its true substance often resides within networks—relationships that carry influence, confer protection, and create advantage long before any formal transaction takes place. Among those who preserve capital across generations, connections are not ornamental; they are infrastructure. They act as conduits for opportunity and as buffers when markets fail to reward timing or merit. Financial capital is counted; social capital is trusted. And when crises, transitions, or reinventions arrive, it is often the latter that proves decisive.

Popular narratives romanticise wealth as a solitary pursuit: the visionary founder, the brilliant investor, the iconoclastic outsider who defied odds. Yet wealth that endures almost never moves alone. It circulates in dense, selective, informal networks that function as a parallel economy. At the apex of influence, access is granted not by credentials alone, but through credibility, embedded trust, and years—sometimes decades—of cultivation. When vulnerability strikes, it is these connections, not public markets or opinion, that provide protection.

The mechanisms are subtle yet formidable. A struggling enterprise receives bridge financing quietly from a peer's family office. A reputational threat is neutralised through coordinated advisory support. A founder exiting a market finds a new opportunity via long-standing allies. These are not random acts; they are triggered by networks operating with the logic of mutual aid—not altruistic, but reciprocal. The wealthy assist one another to remain solvent and resilient, preserving stability within their trusted circles rather than forming overt cartels.

Preservation is not merely reactive; it is deliberate. In private equity, syndication often privileges the group over the individual fund: deals circulate to keep the right participants liquid and successful. Philanthropic contributions reinforce legacy, visibility, and relational debt among peers. Political influence is extended—or withheld—to signal allegiance and future optionality. In each case, the financial benefit flows alongside the social architecture, never apart from it.

To outsiders, these dynamics may appear opaque, even inequitable. Indeed, the rules are uneven. Yet they are rational, grounded in sophisticated game theory: when risk is communal, the rational actor insures not just personal downside but the network's resilience. Elite networks are maintained with discipline: introductions are filtered, behaviour is remembered, reciprocity is tracked informally but consequentially. Breach of trust carries exclusion from opportunities unavailable elsewhere.

The leverage of these networks is often invisible. A high-net-worth individual joining a cultural board signals legitimacy and proximity within the class. A family office co-investing in a minor venture is often prioritising access to the deal flow, not the underlying asset. In crises—liquidity squeezes, legal challenges, reputational threats—it is not the bank hotline that matters, but who answers the call without prompting.

Insiders sometimes refer, half-jokingly, to a "downturn phone tree." During macro shocks—2008, 2020, or sudden regulatory shifts—these networks activate in a coordinated rhythm. Liquidity circulates along trusted lines, advisors mobilise discreetly, government channels are consulted, asset repricing is negotiated in ways that favour insiders. This is not conspiratorial; it is continuity. While the average investor reacts to headlines, those embedded in the network gain time, space, and strategic calm.

Understanding social capital as financial capital requires grasping its underlying currencies. Credibility is earned through performance, preserved through discretion. Generosity matters, but only when coupled with reliability. Status is useful, but only if exercised with tact. Visibility in the right circles outweighs public fame. The ultra-wealthy maintain a low public profile yet a high profile where it truly counts: closed investor forums, selective cultural sponsorships, family office summits.

This relational infrastructure fosters anti-fragility. Individual failures—business collapses, scandals, public setbacks—rarely compromise the network. Diversified ties, distributed favours, and layered reputational structures allow the ecosystem to absorb shocks, reallocate resources, and continue functioning despite isolated breakdowns.

Crucially, social capital is not static. It demands maintenance, pruning, and renewal. Transactional use—calling only when needed, failing to reciprocate, or over-leveraging access—leads to marginalisation. Unlike financial portfolios, social capital requires active stewardship. Dynasties invest in cultivating the next generation's embeddedness: elite schooling, cultural sponsorships, mentorships. The objective is not exposure alone but integration.

Much of what occurs in these networks is invisible to the public. Mergers discussed over dinner, real estate opportunities whispered in private clubs, capital calls met quietly—none leave a digital trace. Yet these exchanges shape wealth trajectories for decades. Public markets are only a partial map; the true frontiers of capital are navigated through trust, conversation, and credibility.

Treating relationships as financial instruments is more than metaphor. They yield not in basis points but in deal access, downside protection, and information asymmetry. They carry informal obligations and offer portfolio-like diversification: reputational capital in one sector can unlock opportunities in another. A hedge fund manager respected in philanthropy gains access to endowment money; a tech founder mentoring peers becomes the first call on a secondary opportunity. These are not coincidences; they are compounded social returns.

This chapter explores that hidden world with precision and nuance. It examines how the wealthy construct relational ecosystems and deploy them strategically and tactically, creating advantages that money alone cannot provide. For anyone seeking to understand enduring wealth, this knowledge is not optional. At the highest echelons of capital, the fastest-moving, most signalling, and most protective currency is not printed—it is earned, remembered, and judiciously shared. Its value lies not merely in counting it, but in cultivating it.

Relationships as Financial Instruments

Few things accrue compound value like trust. In the financial world, capital may scale through leverage, interest, or appreciation—but social capital, when understood and cultivated with intent, can yield returns across dimensions that money alone cannot access. For the wealthy, elite relationships often function like equity: built slowly, valued asymmetrically, and deployed strategically—not merely to gain, but to preserve, protect, and pivot. These relationships are not superficial networks; they are economic instruments cloaked in the texture of personal rapport. *To the enduring rich, relationships are not optional embellishments—they are structured assets.*

Unlike cash or stock, the value of a relationship lies not in its liquidity but in its elasticity. It protects the downside, smooths volatility, and, in moments of constraint, creates access others simply cannot buy. While retail investors chase alpha in public markets, the affluent quietly cultivate relational portfolios—lawyers who become informal risk advisors, art dealers who whisper the right time to buy or sell, fund managers who phone first before the memo circulates. These are not transactions. They are embedded privileges granted only through long-maintained trust.

It is common to speak of "who you know" as an advantage, but the wealthy treat this far less casually. To them, "who you know" is *what* you own—deployed with the same intentionality as any private equity fund or strategic land bank. When George Soros faced a major liquidity squeeze in 1987, it was not his trading algorithm or fund performance that steadied his position, but a handful of relationships with European private banks who extended him crucial flexibility before the dust settled. They acted not on spreadsheet analysis, but on decades of familiarity with his integrity and discipline under stress. *This is capital that cannot be modelled, only earned.*

One of the clearest expressions of relational equity is access. Private markets, by definition, are inaccessible to the general public. But access is not simply about inclusion—it is about *sequence.* The rich often arrive early, sometimes at the formation stage of deals, long before headlines or valuations surface. A $20 million family office may sit quietly on a seed cap table, invited not merely for its funds, but for the credibility and cascade of relationships it brings with it—future distribution partners, press insulation, diplomatic pathways. Their cheque is a signal. Their presence, strategic.

These networks are self-sustaining. Like tightly woven fibres, they reinforce one another structurally. In Silicon Valley, for instance, a handful of tech founders and venture capitalists regularly exchange introductions, pre-screened deal flow, and strategic favours not because of transactional need, but because each maintains a long-view mindset: *what benefits one today strengthens the fabric for all tomorrow.* This is informal reciprocity with hard consequences. An LP who co-invests today might grant preferential allocation next quarter; a founder rescued with bridge capital might later steer a $100 million exit through the network.

Such dynamics are particularly visible during downturns. During the 2008 financial crisis, several ultra-wealthy investors bypassed frozen capital markets by activating dormant networks—calling in informal debts, organising silent equity rescues, coordinating PR offensives through connected media houses. These weren't reactive lifelines. They were pre-structured moves, built into the fabric of long-term alliances. Many family offices operate with quiet contingency protocols: *who to call first if a portfolio asset is under activist attack, who can neutralise litigation exposure without triggering press, who can arbitrage reputation swiftly before media narratives ossify*. This is *liquidity of influence*, not liquidity of funds.

The assumption that wealthy networks are closed systems driven solely by self-interest misses the nuance. *Yes, gatekeeping is real*, and the circulation of opportunity is intentionally curated. But within the gates, the currency is trust—trust not as sentiment, but as a history of fulfilled obligations, quality of judgement, and behavioural consistency across cycles. The wealthy may introduce someone to a deal not because of direct benefit, but because the person's presence reduces aggregate risk. Inclusion, then, is often a strategic hedge.

The language of elite relationships is also notably different. Fewer contracts, more handshakes. Less reliance on arbitration, more expectation of discretion. This is not casual informality; it is a form of legal design: *social contracts fortified by mutual reputational risk*. Breach them, and you're not merely excluded from one deal—you are softly erased from the system that fed you access in the first place.

Interestingly, these networks are increasingly multigenerational. Some family offices actively groom successors not just in investment acumen but in *relational stewardship*—ensuring that the next generation doesn't merely inherit wealth but maintains the relational architecture that sustains it. A grandson who is brash with a senior banker might burn a line of access that took two generations to develop. As one private client advisor described: "Wealth without relational memory is fast capital. And fast capital is what disappears first under pressure."

Contrast this with how most people treat relationships: occasionally instrumental, loosely maintained, and often reactive. This difference in intentionality is profound. The rich engineer their networks with the same foresight they apply to asset allocations. They know a legal case might not hinge on the strength of facts, but on the quiet phone call made to the right intermediary before the case escalates. They understand that a strategic endorsement at the right moment from a well-regarded peer might open a boardroom or block a hostile takeover. *These are intangible derivatives—soft power instruments priced in discretion and leverage.*

One area where this becomes especially visible is the philanthropic sphere. Major donors do not merely give; they *signal.* Donating early to a flagship project at a prestigious university or museum isn't just generosity—it is a form of positioning. These acts create *relational liquidity* with institutions that may, one day, control naming rights, influence zoning decisions, or shape regulatory conversations. The return isn't monetary—it's structural influence.

To mistake this as elitism misses the architecture. In financial markets, a prime broker relationship is different from a retail bank account—not because one is morally superior, but because the relationship *enables action* under very different terms. So too in social capital: relationships among the wealthy carry a different volatility profile. They may not yield every quarter. But they can be activated precisely when needed most.

In this way, relationships become one of the most unrecognised and underpriced financial assets in a wealthy individual's portfolio. They enable illiquidity when needed, access when strategic, and soft landings when abrupt correction is unavoidable. They accrue value quietly but compound influence relentlessly.

Understanding this transforms how we think about capital. It's not merely a matter of asset classes and risk tolerance. It's about *relational positioning: who trusts you to act well, speak discreetly, move early, or withdraw honourably.* If you are trusted on these fronts, you possess a form of embedded equity that no market volatility can erode. Relationships, when viewed with such clarity, are not just the soil in which financial opportunity grows—they are the scaffolding that keeps the structure from collapsing.

Gatekeeping and the Circulation of Opportunity

In the upper reaches of wealth and influence, opportunity does not flow evenly or randomly. It circulates—intentionally, selectively, and often invisibly—within tightly managed ecosystems. Contrary to the ideal of meritocracy that underpins much of the popular narrative around success, elite circles operate according to subtler, more curated logics. Access is not only about ability; it is about proximity. Talent is necessary, but rarely sufficient. At the apex of financial and social capital, *who hears about what, when, and from whom* shapes outcomes as much as what they do with that information.

The mechanics of elite gatekeeping are neither accidental nor uniformly nefarious. They are designed to concentrate advantages among those who already possess them—not always maliciously, but often as a matter of preservation, trust, and shared language. In this world, trust is a currency more valuable than cash. The circulation of deal flow, job offers, insider intelligence, and privileged invitations is not a democratic process—it's a gate-kept one. And the gates are rarely visible.

What makes these networks powerful is not just their exclusivity but their strategic filtration. A promising investment opportunity, for example, doesn't travel through public platforms or retail investor channels. It moves through dinner parties in Mayfair, closed WhatsApp groups of former McKinsey partners, or a golf weekend in Jackson Hole. By the time the public hears about it—if they ever do—the terms have changed, the upside has compressed, and the risk has shifted. *Being early*, in this world, is often just a matter of being inside.

These circulations don't just govern financial opportunities. They determine career mobility, media visibility, philanthropic alignments, and access to legal or reputational defence mechanisms. A single favourable introduction can yield decades of downstream benefit; one exclusion can lock an outsider out for good. The illusion of equal access—of open calls and fair competition—coexists with a reality where many of the most valuable chances never surface publicly. They are passed hand-to-hand, inside what Pierre Bourdieu might have called "fields of power," through rituals that feel social but function economically.

Consider the role of social clubs and private alumni networks—not as sites of leisure, but as infrastructures of economic curation. When a partner at a top venture capital firm shares a deal with a fellow Oxbridge graduate at a private members' club, this is not friendship—it's *resource transfer disguised as sociality*. The mechanisms may appear soft, but the effects are hard and measurable. Entire markets shift based on who is allowed into these informal loops and who is not. Careers are fast-tracked or invisibilised. Companies survive or collapse.

The irony is that this circulation, though deeply strategic, is often cloaked in the language of coincidence. "We happened to meet at a conference." "I thought you two should know each other." "I'm just connecting good people." These phrases obscure the fact that most high-value connections are not random. They are deliberately engineered, or at the very least, channelled through curated filters. Serendipity at this level is rarely unplanned.

Gatekeeping in elite circles isn't only about maintaining social homogeneity—it's also a risk-management function. Who is allowed in, who gets trusted, who is handed access to sensitive information or fragile deals, depends on perceived reputational predictability.

This is why many of the world's most connected individuals maintain what seem like unusually conservative public personas. *The cost of scandal, or even eccentricity, is exclusion.* And exclusion is not just social—it is economic.

That's why the game is not simply about getting access, but staying eligible. To move through these gates requires a fluency in soft codes: discretion, non-neediness, reciprocal value, and contextual awareness. Even among the ultra-wealthy, social capital is tiered. There is a difference between being rich and being *networked-rich*—between owning assets and being part of the architecture through which future assets are decided.

Take the circulation of early-stage tech investments. When a founder raises a pre-seed round, the round is typically oversubscribed before a single public pitch is made. Access is granted to individuals who have been *pre-approved*—those with reputation capital, adjacent investments, and relevance to the founder's vision. This is not about meritocracy; it's about *cohesive signalling.* A well-known angel investor's presence on a cap table isn't just money—it's an endorsement, a credibility layer, a gateway to further resources. And that investor only received the offer because they had been circulating in the right rooms, over the right dinners, at the right time.

The employment world is no different. The phrase "the job was never posted" is not a rare anecdote—it's the default mode at elite levels. Executive hires, media appointments, board seats—these rarely stem from cold applications. They are passed along, whispered about, and quietly aligned before any public announcement. To the outsider, this looks like seamless ascent. To the insider, it is the output of years of network cultivation, signal alignment, and subtle credential stacking.

Information flow operates on similar lines. Access to early macroeconomic data, to company missteps before they hit the news, or to soft intelligence about geopolitical shifts—these data points move quickly, but selectively. This doesn't always mean insider trading in the legal sense; it often means being *close to people who know things before others do.* That proximity becomes arbitrage. The market may be efficient, but the flow of data into that market is not.

None of this suggests that skill, effort, or innovation are irrelevant. But in elite circles, *those qualities are table stakes.* What separates the merely excellent from the systemically advantaged is not performance alone—it is participation in high-trust loops. These loops are policed, maintained, and fiercely protected. And to gain entry requires more than competence. It requires endorsement by a node already inside.

This leads to a structural paradox: the tools that optimise resource flow at the top also obscure opportunity from below. Networks are efficient for those inside them but opaque to those outside. This opacity is not accidental—it is a feature, not a bug. Transparency dilutes advantage. So information, once identified as valuable, becomes privatised. What was once public becomes closed. What was once merit-based becomes trust-based.

Understanding this dynamic is not about moral outrage or resigned cynicism—it's about realism. *The structure of elite gatekeeping is one of the most powerful force multipliers of persistent wealth.* It ensures that opportunity is not just earned—it is inherited socially, even when not inherited financially. It makes financial capital reproducible not just through money, but through *relational position.*

This is why strategic networking is not superficial—it is foundational. It's not about visibility, but *precision connection.* The most valuable introductions are not the ones that earn likes on LinkedIn. They are the ones no one sees. And they are often *never made for free.* Elite networks operate on a give-to-receive economy. If you cannot offer utility, you cannot stay inside the gate.

There is a lesson here for those looking to preserve or build wealth beyond mere investment portfolios. *The architecture of access matters.* If you are not designing your time, presence, and value around proximity to decision-makers, you are depending on luck. And luck, unlike elite networks, is not reproducible.

Those who control the gates do more than open or close them. They shape what happens behind them. And unless you understand the mechanics of circulation—the timing, the trust, the etiquette—you remain downstream of opportunity, reacting rather than participating. The future of capital is not just financial. It is *relationally governed.* Knowing this changes how you think about strategy—not just what you know or do, but *who trusts you enough to tell you first.*

How the Rich Help Each Other Stay Rich

Stability in the upper echelons of wealth is not merely the result of shrewd investing or inherited capital—it is underwritten by a rarely discussed infrastructure of mutual reinforcement. Among the truly wealthy, volatility is buffered not only through assets but through relationships designed for implicit reciprocity. These informal systems—unwritten, often unspoken—serve as a backchannel of support, opportunity, and insulation. When analysed with clarity, they resemble a form of decentralised insurance: reputation-backed, high-trust, and remarkably resilient. *Wealth is less fragile when embedded in a network that has a vested interest in its preservation.*

Unlike the broader economy, where individuals typically fend for themselves during downturns, the affluent operate within a lattice of mutually beneficial favours and informal covenants. These do not function like traditional contracts, but they are enforced by something arguably stronger than legality: reputation. In elite circles, social capital and financial capital are often indistinguishable, each reinforcing the other. *The more trusted you are, the more opportunities flow your way—and the more protected you become when circumstances tighten.* It is this dynamic that keeps the upper class not only solvent, but strategically advantaged when others are forced to retreat.

Consider the quiet resilience of legacy families during financial crises. When markets convulse, they are not scrambling to meet margin calls or renegotiating debt covenants in isolation. Instead, bridge financing comes from a cousin's fund. Legal threats are neutralised by a lawyer in the family office network. Discreet public relations teams step in to soften reputational damage. These interventions are not framed as favours in the conventional sense. They are repayments of past support—or investments in future influence.

There is no ledger, but the memory is long. *Trust, in this economy, is a multi-generational currency.*

The structure of this informal reciprocity often mirrors a closed-loop system. Within it, capital, opportunity, and protection circulate among a fixed set of players. Not everyone gets access. Not every request is granted. But among those who qualify—typically via wealth, credibility, or kinship—the safety net is both broad and deep. The fact that this infrastructure is rarely visible to outsiders is not incidental; it is by design. Publicity dilutes efficacy. And more importantly, *visibility invites regulation, resentment, or unwanted participation.*

To see this system in motion, look at private investment deals. Many never make it to market. Before public listings or even formal fundraising, elite investors are often granted "first look" privileges—early access to opportunities precisely because they have *either delivered value before or are expected to in future.* Similarly, when a business collapses, the founder with strong elite ties is less likely to face personal ruin. Debt is quietly refinanced. Advisors are deployed to restructure. A "strategic acquisition" is floated before liquidation becomes a headline. None of this is guaranteed. But among the wealthy, *failure is often softened—not by systems of state support, but by the informal infrastructure of peer capital.*

This doesn't only happen in finance. It appears in careers, too. A former hedge fund manager loses regulatory approval to manage client money. Months later, he's working as a high-paid advisor at a related firm—one founded by a former protégé. The network protects its own. Not out of sentiment, but out of an understanding that *preserving the competence and dignity of members serves the network's overall strength.* In these settings, social capital compounds. Past alliances become future insurance. Reciprocity is not merely goodwill—it's strategic.

This logic also governs the flow of information. Insider knowledge, for legal and ethical reasons, is tightly monitored in public markets. But soft intelligence—like knowing when a key executive is about to step down, or which regulator is shifting enforcement priorities—is passed along in informal circles. The wealthy are not simply buying stocks or companies. They are *buying better vantage points from which to make decisions*, and those vantage points are often shaped by access to high-trust, high-leverage information. The result? A faster feedback loop, a more nuanced sense of timing, and, crucially, *the ability to act before others even know a shift is underway.*

What makes these systems so enduring is that they are self-reinforcing. Those inside the circle benefit from collaboration, which increases their advantage. Those outside are often unaware they exist—or lack the means to enter. This doesn't mean every elite circle is closed or malicious. But it does mean that *opportunity flows differently when one is structurally connected to others with resources, reach, and readiness to intervene.*

Reciprocity among the rich also thrives because it is rarely zero-sum. A billionaire offering a six-month office space loan to a struggling peer doesn't meaningfully lose anything. But the recipient may avoid costly downsizing, protect employee morale, and recover faster. The cost to the giver is marginal. The gain to the receiver is massive. These asymmetries make generosity among elites easier to sustain—because the capital outlay is small, but the social return is large. *And in a world where long-term influence is more valuable than short-term cash, such exchanges are seen as prudent, not charitable.*

Some might argue this is simply how relationships should work at all levels of society. And to a degree, that's true. But what distinguishes elite reciprocity is not its sentiment but its *strategic architecture*. These networks are cultivated with patience, maintained with discretion, and activated with precision. It's not about having a broad network—it's about having the *right nodes with the right incentives.*

A final insight worth underscoring: these informal systems are not immune to erosion. When trust decays, when members exploit rather than reinforce, the structure weakens. That's why, paradoxically, some of the wealthiest people are also *among the most careful in their social dealings*. A reputation for unreliability in elite circles can quietly but decisively end one's access to these informal safety nets. *The real cost of betrayal is not punishment—it is exclusion.*

To understand how the rich stay rich is to understand that capital is only part of the equation. *The other part is connectivity—who can be called when the storm hits, and who will answer.* These systems may never show up in financial statements, but they are no less real. They are the quiet scaffolding beneath visible success. And they remind us that in high finance, as in life, *who you know is not just useful—it's protective.*

The Downturn Phone Tree

When crisis strikes, most people reach for liquidity, cut losses, and hope to survive. The elite—those with structural access to capital, connections, and discretion—reach for the phone. Not the hotline to customer support or the bank manager's queue, but a chain of carefully cultivated allies, each capable of deploying capital, expertise, or narrative control at a moment's notice. This isn't panic—it's choreography. The real advantage of wealth is not merely financial insulation. *It is the speed and precision with which elite networks mobilise to suppress damage, reprice assets, and pre-empt reputational decay.*

The term "downturn phone tree" is not a metaphor. It is a behavioural reality among financially powerful individuals and institutions, where informal calls precede official announcements, and where *what you know before the headlines hit often determines whether you're hit at all.* Market crises don't level the playing field—they reveal the contours of information asymmetry, resource mobility, and relationship durability.

Consider the 2008 financial crisis. While much of the public waited in line at collapsing banks or watched their pensions implode, select hedge funds and family offices were already on private calls—swapping distressed assets at off-market prices, arranging bridge financing for favoured partners, and discreetly coordinating messaging strategies. Not because they had inside information in the regulatory sense, but because they had *inside positioning.* These weren't institutions scrambling—they were people with pre-vetted lists, liquidity contingencies, and reputational allies ready to activate.

A downturn, in elite circles, doesn't merely destroy value—it reallocates it. Who gets to pick up discounted equity, recapitalise distressed ventures, or reposition in a shifting narrative depends less on courage and more on *access.* That access is rarely impersonal. It moves through trust: built not just over dinners or shared alma maters, but through decades of quiet collaboration, favours granted, and reputations tested in private.

Bridge loans are one of the most common instruments deployed during these moments. Publicly, they may appear as sudden injections of capital or "white knight" investments. Privately, they are favours traded on the understanding that today's liquidity provider may require tomorrow's regulatory buffer or business opportunity. These loans are not necessarily profit-maximising in the short term. They're *relationship-maximising.* Protecting a fellow elite from fire-sale conditions today often means ensuring that same ally will pick up your call when the press turns on you, or when you need a partner to absorb reputational risk.

Another tactic common in the elite playbook is the "friendly sale." A business facing public scrutiny or looming insolvency doesn't collapse—it gets quietly absorbed. Not through open bidding, but via closed-door negotiation with trusted buyers who preserve brand integrity and keep skeletons in closets. These sales preserve not just financial value, but *narrative control.* Who the buyer is, how the sale is framed, and what is left unsaid can mean the difference between a dignified pivot and a public scandal.

The same dynamic applies in public relations. When volatility threatens brand equity, the average firm hires a crisis comms agency. But the truly wealthy activate what amounts to a reputational syndicate. These are not merely firms under retainer, but individuals embedded across media, legal, and regulatory landscapes. The value here is not just in spin—it's in *selective silence, delay, or reframing.* A controversial investment becomes "strategic repositioning." A regulatory probe becomes "industry review." And crucially, damaging stories often don't get published at all. Not because of censorship, but because key stakeholders understand that today's exposure risks tomorrow's access.

These protective moves are rarely dramatic. They are intentionally subdued, orchestrated for minimum attention and maximum control. The key is to move *before* panic sets in. And this is where the phone tree becomes most effective—not just as a reactionary tool, but as a *predictive intelligence network*. If three trusted contacts mention a potential regulatory shift, a market trend, or a liquidity crunch in the same week, action is taken. Portfolios are hedged. Leadership statements are drafted. Exit clauses are quietly triggered. *By the time the public reacts, the elite have already rebalanced.*

To outsiders, this may sound conspiratorial. In practice, it's just systems design. The wealthy understand what most do not: that *chaos is not evenly distributed.* The first wave of losses hits those without buffers—those who wait for the market to react instead of shaping it. Elites do not wait. They coordinate.

Coordination, however, requires frictionless trust. That's why these networks tend to be small, tightly curated, and slow to admit newcomers. It's not about exclusion for its own sake. It's about *credibility, discretion, and reciprocity.* The phone tree only works if every node can be counted on to act in aligned self-interest—not to leak, hesitate, or grandstand. Members are selected not for wealth alone, but for *reliability under stress.*

There's a deeper philosophical insight here: *resilience at the highest levels is not individual, but networked.* The illusion of the self-made billionaire often collapses under scrutiny. What remains is an architecture of quiet dependencies—well-managed, high-leverage relationships that activate when needed and recede when not.

This dynamic is often most visible in succession events. When an elite founder dies or exits, their phone tree is inherited. Not automatically, but intentionally. The heir is introduced, socialised, and tested over time. The transfer of wealth is not the hard part; the transfer of *relational capital* is. It is this capital that determines whether the downturn phone tree will still answer your calls.

During COVID-19's early panic phase, for instance, certain luxury brands and private conglomerates appeared eerily well-positioned. Their supply chains rerouted faster. Their liquidity held. Their brand reputations remained intact. The reason? Weeks before lockdowns, private calls had already passed through the networks—*not just alerting members, but mobilising responses.* Warehouses were pre-stocked.

PR teams drafted crisis language. Internal comms were stress-tested. Competitors without these networks reacted late and paid dearly.

None of this is accidental. It is the outcome of sustained investment—not just in financial vehicles, but in *human infrastructure.* The elite don't just diversify portfolios; they diversify alliances. They think in decades, not quarters. And they understand that when systems fail, it is *your weakest relationship, not your riskiest asset*, that determines your survival.

In summary, the downturn phone tree is not a charming metaphor for camaraderie among the elite. It is a strategic operating system—silent, swift, and calibrated to protect advantage before headlines even suggest danger. For those within its reach, crises are not moments of exposure but of opportunity: to consolidate, to acquire, to pivot without spectacle. For those outside it, the playing field remains uneven—*not because of bad luck, but because the game began before they even saw the scoreboard.*

Chapter 7
Information Asymmetry

Information is never evenly distributed, nor is the power that comes with it. This is not a philosophical observation on fairness; it is a practical description of how modern capital preservation functions. Popular imagination tends to assume that financial success stems from superior decision-making under shared conditions—same markets, same headlines, same rules. In truth, the most enduring wealth is built on staggered timing, privileged access to filtered data, and the ability to act before consequences reach public attention. The truly wealthy do not merely react to markets—they anticipate them, operating within structurally advantaged informational environments. Grasping how this asymmetry is engineered, maintained, and leveraged is essential to understanding why the wealthy remain wealthy.

What most people consume as "news" is, for many elite investors and institutions, already dated intelligence. Market shifts, regulatory actions, or asset revaluations often appear sudden in the public eye, but they are typically the tail end of private sequences: confidential briefings, calls from regulators, or internal memos circulated well in advance. By the time the story hits headlines, capital has moved, hedges have been executed, and reputational narratives carefully pre-positioned. The space between knowledge and consequence is precisely where elite preservation strategies unfold.

This is not about conspiracies—it is about structurally legal, institutionally embedded advantages that favour the top fraction of capital holders. Consider private banking divisions at global financial firms: clients are offered not only bespoke products, but also early insight into policy shifts, geopolitical developments, and macroeconomic indicators, often drawn from intelligence-sharing networks with governments, think tanks, or academic experts. Such information is not accessible via Bloomberg terminals or public filings. It is shared verbally, off-record, through trusted advisory channels. These arrangements are neither illicit nor secretive—they are simply unavailable to those outside the ecosystem.

A concrete example illustrates the point. When European regulators were revising solvency ratios for mid-sized banks following a Southern European debt crisis, certain family offices quietly adjusted their positions months before any media mentioned systemic risk. These actions were informed by lawyer-mediated briefings, informal guidance from supervisory authorities, and early drafts of regulatory language reviewed under stakeholder consultation. By the time headlines appeared, panic had already engulfed the uninformed, while those with early access had long since navigated exposure.

This asymmetry extends beyond macroeconomics. It thrives wherever public data lags reality: farmland zoning, supply chain recalibrations, large-scale labour disputes. Where ordinary investors see volatility, the elite recognise narrative maturation. They interpret not only price movements, but the sequence and timing of information. Often, the real value lies in knowing what will be known next.

Media silence is rarely conspiratorial; more often it is the result of carefully calibrated timing. A law firm managing a multi-billion-dollar settlement may delay filings until key parties are briefed. Distressed sales may be masked through off-balance-sheet structures or quiet resignations. The intent is not deception—it is control. Less noise means more time, and time multiplies advantage.

Elite investors pay handsomely for this discretion, building advisory ecosystems akin to diversified portfolios: lawyers attuned to regulatory foresight, consultants with embedded industry intelligence, accountants anticipating litigation trends before they surface. They purchase not generic advice, but foresight curated through trust, domain expertise, and discretion. A mid-level partner, unseen by public media, may shape asset allocations across family offices through a single timely insight.

Such layered advisory structures create nonlinear compounding of informational advantage. When multiple advisors each provide marginally better intelligence than the public, and these insights are acted upon sequentially rather than in isolation, the outcome is exponential. Over years, this allows capital to sidestep volatility traps—panic selling, overreaction, delayed rebalancing—while ordinary investors bleed through friction. Where others stumble, the well-advised move first.

Timing amplifies knowledge into lasting advantage. Two investors might have equal insight into an impending downturn; the one who receives the signal twelve days early can unwind leverage, adjust exposure, and brief stakeholders, while the other reacts under duress. The delta of timing becomes the delta of outcome—not because one knew more, but because one could act without public scrutiny.

Information asymmetry is dynamic, continuously rebalanced by positioning, access, and agility. The wealthy maintain it through long-term advisory relationships, paying not for consensus but for signal, and acting in ways often invisible until outcomes appear inevitable. Timing is reputational too: the ability to pivot discreetly preserves image continuity. A pre-emptive sale before scandal may appear prescient; in reality, it is access. Those without it act last, often seeming panicked, not incompetent.

This system is reinforced daily within high-trust ecosystems. Gatekeepers—lawyers, bankers, consultants—naturally filter and channel quality intelligence to those who cultivate long-term partnerships rather than transactional interactions. A feedback loop emerges: early access attracts more early access. The wealthy are not innately gifted—they are structurally closer to the signal.

It is tempting to assume that wealth preservation results from superior decision-making under equal conditions. In reality, the conditions themselves are unequal, particularly at the informational layer. This chapter unpacks how that inequality operates, who maintains it, and why it shapes market behaviour and the persistence of capital across generations. The goal is not to lament disparity, but to analyse its mechanics with precision. To understand enduring wealth, one must first understand what is known, when it is known, and who is told first.

What the Wealthy Know Before You Do

There is a fundamental asymmetry in how information flows across the economic spectrum. It is not only a matter of wealth disparity, but of temporal advantage—who knows what, and crucially, *when.* Time, in finance, is a multiplier. Early access to meaningful data—before it is publicly priced into markets, before it becomes newsworthy, before regulatory filings make it searchable—can quietly create structural wealth. And this temporal lead, repeated consistently, becomes a private compounder more potent than any single investment thesis. The wealthy do not merely accumulate capital; they accumulate *context faster.*

To grasp how this plays out in practice, consider how investment decisions are made at the institutional level. A public investor hears about a distressed debt opportunity after the media spotlight turns to a crumbling company. By that point, the real gains have been harvested in private. Family offices, hedge fund principals, and ultra-high-net-worth individuals are often briefed days—or weeks—prior via boutique advisory channels, legal counsel, or direct dialogue with credit desks and restructuring teams. They hear the murmurs when the surface is still calm. This early murmur—an unpaid invoice here, a covenant breach there—does not reach the screens of retail investors or even mainstream analysts. But it echoes clearly through the corridors of private wealth.

Information inequality isn't always sinister. It's often procedural. Private clients of investment banks are tiered. Top-tier clients receive advance macroeconomic briefings, private white-glove economic outlooks, and access to structured deals that are never marketed to the public. In many jurisdictions, this is all perfectly legal—because what's being traded isn't insider information, it's *insider positioning.* To be clear, legality is not always congruent with fairness. But this structural imbalance means the wealthy operate in a data layer that floats above the average investor's field of vision. And like tectonic movements, those with instruments to detect early shifts can exit or enter positions before volatility becomes visible.

Legal and tax advisory structures offer another underappreciated conduit of anticipatory insight. When tax law changes are being drafted—well before they're enacted—multinational law firms often consult with their top clients to prepare compliant strategies. The result? Those at the top are not only ready; they've often *benefited* from transitional loopholes the legislation inadvertently creates. When the new rules finally reach public consciousness, they arrive at the desks of the affluent not as threats, but as tailwinds already priced into their forward strategy.

This isn't about insider trading in the cinematic sense; it's about institutionalised early warning systems. Consider the architecture of wealth offices: a well-structured family office doesn't simply hold assets. It tracks global macro shifts, political elections, weather derivatives, commodity supply chains, and legislation across multiple continents. These offices subscribe to costly geopolitical risk assessments, proprietary research, and invite ex-diplomats and central bankers for private briefings. The point is not just to react but to *pre-act*. And that one-letter difference is what separates protection from prediction.

Timing, in this ecosystem, is not a reaction to headlines—it is an engineered lead. The 2008 financial crisis is a case study. Months before Lehman Brothers collapsed, several hedge funds and private clients began repositioning portfolios based on signals from credit default swaps and interbank lending rates—signals invisible to everyday investors relying on CNBC or Bloomberg. They were not "smarter" in the traditional sense—they were earlier. When volatility struck, their cash positions, hedged bets, and real asset exposures were already in place. That is the hidden dividend of accelerated information flow.

The 2020 COVID-19 market crash revealed this dynamic again. By mid-February, while most media still focused on isolated outbreaks, global investment firms with Asia-based research teams began reallocating into treasury bonds, volatility hedges, and commodity proxies. The signals were not in plain view—they were gleaned from internal supply chain disruptions, regional travel bans, and hospital inventory patterns in Guangdong and Lombardy. By the time governments announced formal lockdowns, liquidity had already migrated.

It's important to note that these anticipatory moves are rarely dramatic. They often look boring: trimming exposure, rotating into defensive sectors, reallocating into income-generating assets. The signal is not in spectacle—it's in subtlety. The wealthy do not require perfect foresight; they require *sufficient lead time.* And because they operate in an ecosystem where that time advantage is built-in, their risk exposure is often a choice, not a surprise.

Beyond markets, early access extends to private deal flow. Private equity rounds, venture placements, distressed asset sales—these are rarely advertised. Participation is controlled through relationship-driven pipelines. Wealth begets access, and access begets earlier positioning. Even when the broader economy enters a drawdown, these investors can still acquire revenue-generating companies, trophy properties, or discounted equity at prices that others won't see until the recovery is priced in. That's not simply good investing—it's information as leverage.

Then there's the role of human capital—advisory teams that act not merely as executors but as *early detection systems.* A sophisticated wealth holder may have separate advisors for legal structuring, philanthropic trusts, sovereign exposure, art valuation, and macro strategy. These advisors don't just wait for instructions—they monitor shifts, anticipate tax impact, assess policy risk, and report anomalies. In effect, they serve as human sensors, offering composite foresight. The wealthy thus gain a map where others only have compasses.

But none of this is immutable. The takeaway is not that this layer of insight is forever sealed off. Rather, it highlights the *value of building proximity to signal.* For the non-wealthy, this may mean cultivating relationships with subject-matter experts, subscribing to higher-fidelity research, or participating in professional forums where information is debated before it becomes doctrine. It means valuing *context before consensus*—not waiting for news, but learning where news gestates.

The structural advantage of the wealthy is not that they are universally smarter or more disciplined. It's that they are rarely surprised. Their environments are designed to *reduce informational lag.*

And in a system where compounding is disrupted by shocks, managing the latency of knowledge is as critical as the knowledge itself.

Ultimately, access to information is not just a matter of inputs—it is a function of architecture. The architecture of attention. Of networks. Of advisory infrastructure. And of timing mechanisms designed not to predict every turn, but to navigate with less delay. *That* is what the wealthy know before you do. Not just what—but when. And in high-stakes finance, *when* is often the difference between endurance and erosion.

Media Silence and Market Quiet

There is a profound difference between absence of noise and absence of news. In modern financial ecosystems, what goes unsaid is often more revealing than what is loudly declared. Markets are supposed to be efficient, democratising access to price signals, risks, and opportunities. But the reality is far murkier. In practice, the wealthy frequently operate in an informational environment curated by silence—where the muting of data, withholding of insight, and delayed disclosure serve as protective measures. *This silence is not random; it is a feature of the system, not a flaw.*

The financial elite do not simply rely on superior information; they often benefit from the controlled distribution of information itself. Regulatory lags, PR strategies, and soft power relationships with media outlets create what economists would call *asymmetric visibility.* It is not that others lack the tools to find the truth—it's that the truth is made less visible, less urgent, or less believable until the insiders have already acted.

Consider, for instance, the subtle delays in public awareness that accompany distressed corporate restructurings or major insider exits. While a high-profile CEO stepping down is reported in glossy headlines, the real story—the boardroom manoeuvres, hedged trades, or quiet capital withdrawals—may have taken place months earlier, shared only among trusted confidants, legal teams, or board-level intermediaries. By the time the public hears it, the event is priced in, the edge is gone, and the opportunity is already monetised.

This phenomenon has real, systemic consequences. Much of the modern media ecosystem, particularly financial journalism, operates within a tension between access and adversarialism. Outlets that lean too heavily into investigative exposure risk losing privileged relationships with sources and sponsors. The result is a transactional equilibrium: some stories are delayed, softened, or strategically buried to preserve future access. *It is not censorship in the traditional sense; it is omission by incentive.*

Market silence is often engineered not through conspiracy, but through the ambient self-regulation of reputation-sensitive actors. Investor relations officers, legal compliance teams, and corporate PR firms are not just tasked with messaging—they are tactical participants in what information *should not* circulate. When liquidity events are pending, when buybacks are timed to narrative highs, or when legal exposure risks cascading into regulatory scrutiny, *silence becomes strategy.*

Real estate markets offer a pointed example. During periods of downturn, certain institutional investors quietly renegotiate loan covenants, restructure debt, or pre-emptively sell off Class B assets to shore up balance sheets. These moves are not accompanied by press releases. They are executed quietly, often under NDAs, sometimes through layered entities that obscure beneficial ownership. The public narrative may remain bullish on the sector even as the most informed players exit discreetly. *The absence of panic is not a sign of calm—it may be the result of successful concealment.*

Even in highly regulated sectors such as banking, timing disclosures can tilt the playing field. Wealth managers serving ultra-high-net-worth clients may receive pre-emptive guidance about shifts in central bank posture, new regulatory interpretations, or imminent tax reforms—not in the form of leaked memos, but through "client briefings" that carry an implicit advantage. *Discretionary intelligence—when to act, not just what to act on—becomes the true edge.*

During the 2008 financial crisis, for instance, certain hedge funds and family offices moved into distressed credit positions with surgical timing. They were not acting on illegal tips; they were reading the silences. When major banks stopped taking certain positions, when interbank lending subtly froze, when pricing anomalies persisted without commentary—these were not anomalies to be ignored. They were invitations to reallocate, restructure, or retreat. *Market quiet is often an information flare in reverse.*

The wealthy also invest heavily—not just in financial products—but in the insulation of reputation. Media silence is often purchased, indirectly, through philanthropic visibility, board memberships, or quiet partnerships with think tanks and educational institutions. These relationships do not directly buy silence, but they generate a protective halo that can slow negative exposure or redirect critical narratives. A tech founder under antitrust scrutiny may simultaneously fund digital literacy programmes, reshaping their public image just enough to dampen regulatory appetite. The same principle applies in reverse: bad news can be timed for quiet news cycles, dropped on Fridays, or softened through exclusive access to sympathetic journalists. *Managing optics is not merely reputational—it is financial.*

It would be a mistake to assume that media silence always involves malicious intent. Much of it is structurally baked into how elite networks function. Certain deals, for instance, are only viable if conducted under the radar—late-stage private equity transactions, land assembly for megaprojects, or distressed asset repositioning hinge on discretion. The wealthy do not merely seek return on capital—they seek the *optionality of secrecy*. This optionality allows them to test ideas, hedge reputational risk, and operate with fewer eyes on their leverage points.

Consider the legal tactics used during early acquisition phases. Non-disclosure agreements, shell corporations, and staggered filings are not exotic tools; they are commonplace in the upper echelons of capital strategy. By the time a retail investor sees a headline—"Company X acquires Company Y"—the true strategic gain has already been captured: through zoning variances secured in silence, through board-level exits negotiated without public drama, through permits quietly pushed through by law firms with municipal ties. *What the market sees is often the afterglow, not the spark.*

None of this suggests that the wealthy possess absolute control over media or markets. But they do operate within systems designed to grant *temporal advantage*—the ability to move before others even realise a move is necessary. This is not about access to more information; it is about earlier access to *less public* information, and the systemic incentives that preserve that asymmetry. The signal, in their world, is not louder—it is earlier, quieter, and often delivered behind a closed door.

The implications are stark. For most investors, transparency is an after-the-fact event. SEC filings, quarterly earnings, and official press releases are not information—they are confirmation. The real edge lies upstream: in who gets the first whisper, not who reads the final report.

Information asymmetry does not always manifest as fraud, leaks, or malfeasance. Its most powerful form is structural—made invisible by timing, language, and social insulation. *The market may be public, but the game is often private.* To understand how the wealthy stay wealthy, one must listen not only to what is said, but to what is omitted—and why that silence, however polite or procedural, often carries the loudest truth.

Paying for Better Advice

There is a misconception, almost mythological in its persistence, that the ultra-wealthy operate on instinct—gut calls made on yachts and in boardrooms, guided by innate brilliance or entrepreneurial magic. In reality, the rich are more often orchestrators of layered information ecosystems, where access to refined judgement is not only bought but structured with architectural intent. For those who manage vast capital or oversee intricate holdings, advice is not occasional or incidental. It is permanent infrastructure—paid for, selected, tiered, and optimised not to confirm a worldview, but to reveal blind spots the average investor never even knows they have.

This is not advice in the way most people experience it. It's not a meeting with a financial planner once a year or a broker's update on market trends. The wealthy treat advice like a critical asset class. They build advisory layers across legal, regulatory, geopolitical, tax, macroeconomic, real estate, and philanthropic domains—each providing distinct lenses on potential risk and future positioning. Where middle-income professionals seek simplified recommendations—"Should I invest in bonds or equities?"—the wealthy are asking questions two chess moves ahead: "What are the legislative threats to this tax shelter if control of Congress flips?" "How would European Central Bank policy on rate easing affect my exposure to Tier II commercial real estate in Germany?" "Is it worth structuring the acquisition under a private trust in Singapore?"

They don't just want answers; they pay to have better questions posed on their behalf.

One of the least visible, yet most powerful, dynamics in elite wealth preservation is this: superior advice multiplies over time. Like compounding returns, early insights not only prevent mistakes but seed advantages that surface years later in dramatically improved positioning. This may mean structuring holdings to avoid punitive inheritance taxes across jurisdictions or pre-emptively reorganising a business entity ahead of anticipated regulatory tightening. It might mean hedging currency risk before a devaluation that hasn't yet made headlines, or divesting from an industry months before the market collectively downgrades its outlook.

A pivotal reason this advice works is its *customisation*. Off-the-shelf frameworks are fine for retail investors, but for the wealthy—whose risk exposure is asymmetric and whose footprint often spans legal and national boundaries—standard advice is a liability. They require counsel that accounts for privacy needs, reputational sensitivities, and cross-border complexity. And they are willing to pay dearly for it, not just in retainer fees, but in loyalty and influence—sometimes bringing advisors into inner circles where personal and professional interests coalesce. This intimacy gives rise to a different category of advisor: not merely consultant, but consigliere. Someone who doesn't just offer options, but navigates dilemmas.

To appreciate the asymmetry, consider the difference in crisis preparedness. When a market shock hits—say, an unexpected rate hike or a sudden geopolitical escalation—the average investor receives reactive headlines, maybe a panicked call from their broker. The ultra-wealthy, meanwhile, have often been briefed days or even weeks earlier by multi-disciplinary teams watching primary indicators or interpreting diplomatic tea leaves. This isn't illegal insider trading—it's legal, structural informational advantage. Their tax attorney isn't guessing at regulatory shifts; they're in closed-door roundtables with policy analysts. Their macroeconomic advisor isn't reading from the Financial Times; they're running private simulations based on real-time data. Their PR counsel isn't responding to a reputation hit; they're anticipating it with crisis protocols designed in calm, not chaos.

It's this anticipatory posture that sets elite advisory systems apart. In middle-class frameworks, advice is largely backward-looking or compliance-oriented. For the rich, advice is forward-scanning, multi-scenario, and synthetic—pulling in legal, psychological, technical, and political perspectives. For example, a billionaire considering the sale of a majority stake in their logistics firm doesn't just consult an investment banker. They convene a set of advisors across antitrust law, public relations, trade policy, ESG impact, and sovereign wealth appetite. Each speaks from their domain, but their insights are cross-validated in ways that expose contradictions and locate optionality.

What emerges from this is not just insight, but *conviction.* When advice is sufficiently broad and vetted, the wealthy can act with greater clarity and confidence—even when the decision itself is high-risk or ambiguous. This decisiveness is another hidden asset of high-quality advice: it reduces cognitive drag and decision fatigue. Rather than second-guessing a move for months, they execute with speed and coordination. The wealthy buy time not just with money, but with certainty—and certainty is often produced by superior advice.

There is also an intergenerational component to this architecture. Many family offices, especially those managing dynastic wealth, institutionalise advisory roles into the governance structure itself. The next generation isn't just given capital—they inherit advisory relationships designed to train, guide, and challenge them. These aren't passive tutors; they're part of a system designed to replicate resilience. That's why so many ultra-wealthy families operate with boards of directors for their personal portfolios, investment committees for philanthropic work, or legal working groups for succession planning. They build these not out of excess, but because they understand that wealth without judgement is entropy waiting to happen.

And crucially, advice is not sought only when needed. *The rich pay for dormant advice*—counsel that may not be immediately applied, but is cultivated and retained in readiness. This is profoundly different from how most people engage professionals. A middle-income individual sees a tax lawyer in April. The wealthy may have one on retainer year-round, engaged in quarterly planning, not annual reporting. Their advisors are proactive architects, not emergency technicians. The cost of this foresight is high, but the cost of its absence is far higher—especially when mistakes can cascade across generations, public reputations, or regulatory bodies.

It's tempting to dismiss all this as privilege—and yes, it is. But it's also replicable in form, if not in scale. The insight is not that everyone should hire a team of geopolitical analysts; it's that *layered thinking must precede layered advice.* One of the biggest mistakes ambitious professionals make as their income grows is assuming they can out-learn structural complexity. But at a certain threshold of wealth, the game changes: you can no longer "do it yourself." The decision is no longer whether to pay for advice, but whether you're paying for the right kind—uncorrelated, independent, strategically uncomfortable.

In that light, the real lesson of the wealthy isn't that they buy advice. It's that they construct it—*deliberately, structurally, and recursively.* They create layered networks of counsel that aren't just technically sound, but that challenge assumptions, stress-test hypotheses, and expand the range of decisions considered. The ROI isn't always visible in quarterly returns. Sometimes it's revealed in the avoidance of disaster, the elegance of a clean succession, or the discreet closing of a tax exposure no one else ever noticed.

To stay rich, one must think like a system, not a self. And in that system, *advice is not an accessory. It's the scaffolding.*

The Edge of Timing

In capital markets, there is a subtle but profound distinction between having information and knowing *when* to act on it. Most investors obsess over what they know—data, trends, forecasts, expert consensus. But for the elite, the decisive advantage is rarely raw knowledge; it is *timing*. They don't just understand what is happening—they position themselves to act before the implications become obvious to the public. Small differences in entry or exit—measured in months, weeks, sometimes hours—compound into outsized returns, protective buffers, or geopolitical positioning that others only recognise in hindsight. Timing is not intuition; it is often the by-product of layered access, institutional memory, and coordinated readiness. It is the edge that hides in sequence, not substance.

To understand this dynamic, consider the case of Blackstone's real estate pivot post-2008. In the aftermath of the global financial crisis, as commercial real estate values plummeted and traditional lenders froze, Blackstone moved aggressively to acquire distressed property portfolios—especially single-family homes in hard-hit U.S. markets like Phoenix, Atlanta, and Las Vegas. They were not the only ones who *knew* that prices were down. Every headline screamed it. But Blackstone had *structural readiness*—a team already assembled, capital already raised, financing pre-structured, and legal frameworks tested. While others were paralysed by uncertainty or waiting for signals of recovery, Blackstone was executing. By 2015, they had become one of the largest landlords in America, and the downstream returns proved exponential. Their informational advantage was real, but their timing edge—grounded in preparedness and strategic boldness—was what transformed knowledge into dominance.

This is the critical distinction: information becomes leverage only when paired with readiness. Timing isn't just about early alerts—it's about internal velocity. A well-briefed billionaire is not advantaged if their decision-making ecosystem is slow, fractured, or bureaucratic. But elite networks—family offices, hedge funds, private equity firms—are often built for nimbleness. Their legal counsel, financial engineers, and geopolitical analysts aren't siloed; they're synchronised. So when a shift occurs—a tax loophole closes, a commodity trend reverses, a central bank signals—the wealthy are not *deciding* whether to act. They are already mid-execution. The window hasn't opened for them—it's halfway closed behind them.

Take, for example, the use of "quiet capital" to front-run regulatory transitions. In 2020, several billionaires in the renewable energy space quietly repositioned capital into rare earth mineral supply chains—specifically lithium and cobalt—months before global EV mandates accelerated. These bets were not just intuitive plays on green energy; they were carefully timed moves driven by private policy briefings, early signals from European and Chinese legislative blocs, and long relationships with multinational OEMs. By the time retail investors noticed the surge in clean energy ETFs, the elite had already arbitraged the bottlenecks. What mattered wasn't their belief in ESG narratives; it was the timing of their repositioning within that arc.

This strategic front-running is also apparent in sovereign risk management. High-net-worth individuals with global footprints often diversify not just by geography, but by political cycle. In 2012, several Latin American elites began discreetly relocating family assets out of Venezuela and Argentina *before* formal capital controls were imposed. They acted not from panic, but from signals—deteriorating bond yields, judicial reshuffling, informal whispers from regional banks. While others were trapped in frozen currencies or penalised remittance schemes, they had already converted holdings into real estate in Miami, art in London, or trusts in Liechtenstein. Again, the informational signals were subtle—but the real separator was the decisiveness of timing.

Even in highly regulated markets like the United States, timing advantages can operate legally but opaquely. Consider how hedge funds exploit market microstructure. Through relationships with exchanges and brokers, many elite funds receive order flow data milliseconds ahead of execution. This fractional timing, enabled by high-frequency trading algorithms and co-location servers, allows them to arbitrage predictable retail behaviour—buying ahead of large ETF inflows, or shorting just before panic selling escalates. The public sees volatility; the elite see sequences. They profit not from being smarter, but faster—and structurally so.

But timing is not always about speed. Sometimes it's about *waiting*—longer than most people can endure. Ultra-wealthy investors often benefit from the patience that others cannot afford. They can lock up capital for ten years in illiquid vehicles—venture funds, infrastructure projects, or timberland—knowing that the short-term volatility is irrelevant to their goals. In 2011, Yale's endowment doubled down on private equity allocations while peers cut exposure. The decision looked reckless—until the 2015–2020 returns vindicated their contrarian stance. Their timing was not early, but enduring. In this way, the rich enjoy a second timing advantage: *the luxury of detachment from short-term panic.*

This distinction between early and enduring timing is critical. Not all timing edges are about fast reaction. Some are about sustained conviction. In markets saturated by short-termism, the ability to hold unpopular positions through drawdowns becomes a rare form of strategic courage. The wealthy can afford this posture—not just financially, but psychologically. Their portfolios are not built to outperform quarterly benchmarks; they're designed to survive generationally. This design confers a type of temporal insulation that amplifies small advantages over decades, not days.

And still, timing does not exist in a vacuum. It is often downstream from *signal quality.* The wealthy don't just receive information earlier; they receive it with better context. Their advisors don't report facts—they interpret implications. They filter noise from signal with systems built over years: boutique law firms who've seen obscure precedent, former diplomats embedded as policy scouts, data scientists parsing non-public sentiment trends. This networked clarity allows the elite to identify *when* an idea's time has come—not just whether it's true.

A powerful example emerged during the COVID-19 crisis. In January 2020, before global markets recognised the scale of the pandemic, a number of hedge fund managers began shorting hospitality and airline stocks—not in reaction to news headlines, but based on pattern analysis from Wuhan mobility data, informal contacts at medical logistics firms, and private health system analytics. Their actions were weeks ahead of major institutional repositioning. This wasn't clairvoyance; it was sequence fluency. The market caught up in March. The profits were already booked.

This all leads to an uncomfortable truth: in an increasingly transparent world, *opacity has shifted to chronology*. Most investors today have access to the same macroeconomic dashboards, financial statements, and earnings calls. But only some have the structural agility to act ahead of consensus. The edge is not who knows—it's who *moves*, and when. The playbook of the wealthy is less about secret knowledge than about institutional velocity. They don't need better facts. They need faster conviction.

To understand the edge of timing, then, is to understand that timing is not a moment. It is a system: of preparation, signal interpretation, psychological resilience, and coordinated execution. It's the difference between reacting to the market and being the reason the market moves. It's the interval between information and action—where real power lives. The wealthy occupy this interval not by accident, but by design. And that design is what transforms informational asymmetry into structural gain.

Chapter 8
The Psychology of Staying Rich

The curious paradox of wealth is that the more one possesses, the more acutely one behaves as if something is at stake. Not in the public stories of daring ventures or headline-grabbing acquisitions, but in the quiet chambers of private decision-making, where the predominant force is rarely ambition—it is the avoidance of ruin. The genuinely wealthy rarely act as gamblers hoping to double their chips; they operate more like stewards guarding an inheritance, constantly mindful that preservation often outweighs pursuit. Beneath this mindset lies a simple, yet rarely articulated truth: staying wealthy is less about chasing opportunity than it is about managing fear.

Loss aversion, the behavioural economist's classic insight, is not a peripheral curiosity in high-net-worth psychology; it is the operating system. Among ordinary investors, it surfaces as panic selling, overcorrection, or impulsive rebalancing. Among the elite, it is subtler, manifesting as deliberate underexposure, redundant institutional safeguards, legal over-preparedness, and emotional compartmentalisation. What may seem to outsiders as restraint, even stoicism, is often the reflection of a deep, internalised recognition: the psychological sting of loss far exceeds the pleasure of equivalent gain. Once the game has been won, the objective is no longer accumulation—it is endurance.

This explains why some of the most successful investors appear, at first glance, dull. They rarely make headlines with audacious trades or high-profile gambits. Instead, they deploy capital methodically, leverage cautiously, and prize durability over velocity. To the untrained eye, such conservatism may seem uninspired; in truth, it represents a psychological edge: the capacity to resist action precisely when the world feels most urgent. Paradoxically, their advantage often resides in boredom.

The ability to tolerate ambiguity, defer gratification, and weather extended periods of uncertainty is cultivated skill, frequently across generations. Wealthy families institutionalise this trait via governance structures designed to suppress impulsivity. Investment committees replace charismatic traders. Trusts replace individual risk-takers. Multi-year lock-ups prevent panic. Where a typical investor asks, "What can we do now?" the elite ask, "What does inaction protect?"

Outsiders often interpret such discipline as passivity. Yet history demonstrates that deliberate inaction can be the most aggressive strategy. During the dot-com crash of 2000 and again in 2008, a select cohort of investors resisted selling, despite societal pressure, media alarm, and financial drawdowns. Not because recovery was assured, but because their framework was structural, not quarterly. Time was not an obstacle—it was the medium through which returns compounded.

Consider an illustrative example: a mid-century American industrialist whose descendants today oversee a nine-figure family office. In the stagflation of the 1970s, when equities faltered, gold surged, and inflation eroded purchasing power, he did not rotate into commodities or flee the market. He held, rebalanced minimally, and waited. His rationale, documented in family correspondence, was philosophical rather than technical: economic cycles, like weather, are endured, not outguessed. That patience preserved more real wealth than any tactical hedge could have achieved. Sometimes, the most potent move is refusal.

Psychological mastery extends beyond stillness to emotional diversification. Just as financial portfolios are spread across assets to mitigate risk, emotional portfolios buffer identity against market fluctuations. For the wealthy, capital is entwined with status, control, freedom, and self-worth. A portfolio's turbulence can imperil the self. Elite investors counteract this by cultivating multiple identities—philanthropist, board member, parent, entrepreneur, mentor. Should one identity falter, the others remain intact. This multidimensional selfhood functions as a psychological hedge, insulating not merely against market volatility but against the volatility of self.

Family offices formalise these principles. Wealth is deliberately decoupled from singular self-expression. Heirs pursue distinct careers. Philanthropic operations are treated with equal seriousness to investment arms. Foundations are designed not only for efficiency but for psychological diversification. The implicit message is clear: worth is not solely defined by wealth. This cultivation of meaning is subtle, yet enduring.

Another understated strategy is the delegation of anxiety. Ultra-wealthy individuals surround themselves with advisors—not solely to execute strategy but to absorb uncertainty. Portfolio managers, legal teams, macro analysts: these roles function as emotional shock absorbers, carrying vigilance so that principals can focus. To outsiders, this may appear indulgent; in practice, it is structured detachment—a hierarchy of focus that clarifies decision-making.

Perhaps the least recognised tactic is controlled pessimism. While retail investors often default to optimism, hoping each trade or trend will deliver, the wealthy plan as if failure is inevitable. They rehearse bankruptcies, litigation, reputational crises, and liquidity squeezes. They ask, "Who do we call if this fails? Which assets can be liquidated most quickly? What happens if we die?" This anticipatory pessimism liberates. Once the downside is charted and rehearsed, it ceases to dominate imagination. Risk no longer paralyses—they have met it on their own terms.

This inversion—fear generating freedom—distinguishes enduring wealth from fleeting riches. Where the latter chase gain, the former structure against loss. And fear, when translated into system and habit, becomes strategy. It reshapes capital allocation, emotional management, and identity construction, shifting posture from acceleration to preservation, from visibility to longevity.

The evolution of this mindset is generational. First-generation entrepreneurs may still pursue growth, but successors managing trusts and family reputations prioritise continuity. The fear of squandering legacy supersedes the thrill of novelty. While this can introduce its own challenges—entitlement, paralysis, over-correction—it also instils a crucial trait: non-reactivity, the ability to observe and endure without flinching.

Ultimately, understanding why some families endure financially demands more than an analysis of returns. One must examine psychology: invisible guardrails, rituals of restraint, systems separating emotion from action. Beneath every enduring fortune lies a sequence of quiet decisions: to delay, to wait, to withstand. These are not merely tactical moves; they are psychological ones. And it is here—at the intersection of discipline, patience, and fear—that the true craft of staying rich is revealed.

Fear of Ruin > Hope of Gain

If you want to understand the behaviour of those who remain wealthy across generations, look not to ambition, but to anxiety. The conventional narrative assumes that the rich are relentlessly driven by opportunity—the next market, the next venture, the next asymmetric bet. But the reality is more quietly defensive: they are guided far more often by a deep-seated commitment to *not losing* what they have already accumulated. The psychology of preservation—of keeping rather than winning—dominates elite financial behaviour. *Loss aversion* doesn't just show up at the margins; it defines the entire playbook.

For those with little to lose, risk is a lever of mobility. But for those at the top of the wealth pyramid, risk is more often a liability—a door through which ruin quietly walks in. This asymmetry of fear is not weakness; it is institutionalised wisdom. The wealthier the individual or family, the more likely their systems are designed not to chase alpha, but to hedge beta. It is not only that they want to avoid losses—they want to structurally *incapacitate* the possibility of significant loss. And in doing so, they often outperform over time, not because they seek superior returns, but because they eliminate catastrophic drawdowns that others cannot recover from.

This orientation is not theoretical. It shows up in hard structures: in multi-layered trusts, conservative debt ratios, and a deep cultural aversion to leverage for consumption. It shows up in more subtle norms, too: families that refuse to fund vanity projects, opt out of speculative trends, or deliberately under-own volatile asset classes—despite pressure from their advisors or peers. Even philanthropic decisions are often shaped by an underlying calculus of reputation risk. Beneath the surface, the psychological question being asked is rarely "How much can we gain?" but "What would be irreversible if we were wrong?"

One can see this difference clearly when comparing newly rich entrepreneurs with multi-generational families. The former often embrace risk as a badge of identity, celebrating disruption, movement, and bold bets. The latter, while no less ambitious, tend to favour control. They emphasise processes over outcomes, steady compounding over parabolic returns. It is not that they lack exposure to risk—it's that their exposure is actively governed, and their posture is structurally cautious. The mantra is implicit but powerful: *don't jeopardise the engine that created you.*

Behavioural economics provides the academic language for this. Kahneman and Tversky's Prospect Theory, which formalised the concept of loss aversion, demonstrated that losses are experienced more intensely than equivalent gains. But in elite circles, this is more than an intellectual insight—it's a principle of design. Large family offices, for instance, regularly stress-test their portfolios not only against market downturns but against political shifts, liquidity shocks, even legal disputes. They scenario-plan reputational events. They map the ripple effects of personal scandals. They insure everything insurable and diversify the rest. This is not paranoia. It is disciplined paranoia—what one investor called *optimism with guardrails.*

Consider the asset allocation strategies employed by sovereign wealth funds or endowments with multi-century mandates. Their public facing returns often seem conservative, especially when compared to high-flying hedge funds or tech entrepreneurs. Yet their internal mandate is rarely "beat the market"—it is "survive for 100 years." This reframes the calculus entirely. The volatility they avoid may seem like lost opportunity in bull markets. But over full cycles, the lack of ruin becomes a compounding advantage. The goal is not to maximise excitement—it is to *maximise permanence.*

This mentality also affects liquidity preference. Unlike smaller investors who tend to keep reserves for emergencies, wealthy individuals often build *redundancies* across multiple domains. They do not keep a single safety net—they construct layers. Cash equivalents sit in tiered accounts; real estate is not just owned but *unencumbered*; credit lines are pre-negotiated, not sought during crisis. Family members often operate across jurisdictions, providing optionality not just for lifestyle but for risk management. The result is a kind of *meta-liquidity*—not just capital on hand, but access embedded into relationships, structures, and geography.

Risk, in this environment, is not seen as something to be eliminated—that would be naïve. Rather, it is contained. Families that stay wealthy learn to differentiate between *fragile risk* and *robust risk*. Fragile risk is binary: the kind that could zero out an asset or collapse an enterprise. Robust risk is survivable: a drawdown you can hold through, a lawsuit you can absorb, a downturn you are positioned to endure. The discipline lies in knowing the difference—and in refusing to accept fragile risk even when the returns are seductive.

And this discipline often runs counter to market sentiment. During moments of irrational exuberance, when media headlines scream innovation and alpha, when capital floods into meme stocks, cryptocurrencies, or speculative tech, elite capital tends to step back. Not because they lack belief in disruption, but because they distrust euphoria. They have lived long enough—or stewarded enough capital—to know that *bubbles are only visible in hindsight to those who need the lesson.* Those who don't need the lesson have already built systems that prevent exposure at the peak.

Critics sometimes interpret this conservatism as cowardice. They frame the elite as having "lost their edge"—no longer bold, no longer hungry. But this interpretation misses the point entirely. The most powerful move is often *not playing* when the odds are structurally misaligned. It is a different kind of courage—the kind that walks away from attention, ignores the adrenaline, and endures the quiet. *Strategic restraint is not the absence of ambition; it is the reallocation of ambition across time.*

Wealthy families understand that financial systems compound. But they also understand that *errors compound.* A single poor investment rarely destroys a fortune. But unhedged bets, taken repeatedly, without institutional safeguards, create structural fragility. And so they don't eliminate action—they *sequence* it. They build in slowness. Decisions move through committees, processes, and formal reviews. This might seem inefficient, but in high-stakes domains, slowness is a form of signal filtration. It protects the system from being captured by emotion, hype, or individual impulse.

This culture of restraint often extends beyond finance. It influences career decisions, public engagement, even personal relationships. High-net-worth individuals are advised, coached, and reminded—formally and informally—that reputation, legacy, and capital are intertwined. One ill-considered move, amplified by social media or litigation, can create costs that far exceed any financial loss. Hence the proliferation of risk managers, reputation advisors, and security consultants—many of whom are former intelligence officers, legal experts, or behavioural analysts. *The point is not paranoia. It is asymmetric risk management.*

And yet, restraint is not the same as stagnation. Families that survive and grow over generations often do take bold steps. They invest in private equity, fund new ventures, and pursue global expansion. But these moves are *positioned within buffers*. They risk a slice, not the core. They bet from strength, not desperation. And they size their exposure in proportion to what they can afford to lose. It is not the presence of risk that defines intelligent wealth management—it is the *calibration* of risk.

Ultimately, what differentiates those who stay wealthy from those who don't is not just access or strategy—it is worldview. Most people chase upside. The enduringly wealthy manage downside. And that difference, over years, compounds. Because while upside is often cyclical, *ruin is permanent*. It doesn't matter how many good decisions one makes if a single unhedged event can erase the structure. The true elite know this. And they build accordingly.

They do not talk loudly about it. They do not glorify caution in public speeches or investment memos. But quietly, consistently, they practice restraint as a philosophy. Not because they lack the desire to grow, but because they *understand what growth is worth when weighed against permanence*. Fear, when structured correctly, does not shrink possibility. It refines it. And in that refinement lies the secret of longevity.

The Boredom Edge

Financial media tends to lionise the high-octane: the rapid pivots of venture capital, the instant gratification of speculative trading, the breathless thrill of crypto surges. But beneath this spectacle lies a more enduring and uncelebrated skill—*the ability to do nothing interesting for a very long time.* Among the truly wealthy, boredom is not an affliction to be avoided but an asset to be mastered. It is a form of emotional discipline, a psychological edge that filters noise, resists impulse, and multiplies long-term advantage. In wealth strategy—as in endurance sport—*what is dull is often decisive.*

Where most investors seek stimulation or novelty, the affluent cultivate tolerance for delayed feedback and strategic ambiguity. This is neither laziness nor apathy. It is the behavioural infrastructure behind compounding wealth. If risk is the price of opportunity, boredom is often its currency. When examined closely, some of the world's most successful capital allocators distinguish themselves not by the complexity of their models or the novelty of their trades, but by their capacity to *wait.* The long hold. The no-trade decision. The ability to let something quietly accrete value without checking the scoreboard.

This edge is less about information and more about *interior architecture.* It asks: can you remain focused while everyone else is twitchy? Can you hold a position without fidgeting, a thesis without crowd validation? In a world optimised for speed and feedback loops, the capacity to defer gratification is not just a moral virtue; it is a commercial moat. The very traits that win in algorithmic markets—hyper-reaction, constant adjustment, immediate narrative—are inversely correlated with the temperament required for strategic patience. *Boredom-resilience* may be the last great arbitrage.

Consider the construction of enduring wealth vehicles: generational real estate portfolios, long-dated family trusts, private equity secondaries, or niche insurance vehicles. These are not exciting instruments. They do not generate dopamine. They do not make for energetic cocktail party conversation. And yet, they are precisely the instruments that over decades turn passive capital into multi-generational power. The very dullness that alienates the average investor *protects the asset from unnecessary interference.*

Behavioural finance has long noted the tendency of retail investors to underperform their own investments. They buy high, sell low, churn unnecessarily—victims of emotional hijack. What is less explored is the inverse: the quiet machinery by which the wealthy construct systems that make such interference structurally difficult. They don't just avoid boredom—they institutionalise it. They buy into vehicles with lock-ups. They delegate authority to managers bound by mandates that restrict activity. They create constraints not because they are inefficient, but because they *inoculate against restlessness.*

This logic echoes in the private wealth structures of the ultra-rich. Many family offices operate under investment committees that meet quarterly or even semi-annually, avoiding the neurotic twitch of public markets. The slowness is intentional. As one wealth manager privately remarked, "Our job isn't to maximise returns quarter-to-quarter. It's to reduce the number of irreversible mistakes made during periods of emotional compression." In this view, *patience is not passive—it is actively enforced by design.*

To see this edge in action, observe how the wealthy approach venture capital. While headlines tout unicorn deals and explosive exits, seasoned LPs in top-tier funds understand that the real work is *time arbitrage.* Fund lives are structured around 10+ year cycles for a reason: the signal only emerges slowly. There are no shortcuts. The successful investor is often the one who resists the temptation to "pivot," who tolerates years of illiquidity without demanding movement for movement's sake. In this domain, *boredom is synonymous with discipline.*

But this restraint is not confined to private capital. In public markets too, some of the most effective strategies are those that bore. The success of low-turnover index strategies is well established, but even within active management, the most durable performers often share a counterintuitive trait: infrequent action. Terry Smith, often called "Britain's Warren Buffett," is known for an ultra-low turnover style: "Buy good companies, don't overpay, and do nothing." His results suggest that what passes for inactivity is often *a conscious rejection of distraction.*

The challenge, of course, is that boredom feels irresponsible. In the dopamine-fuelled logic of modern life—refresh, respond, optimise—it feels like a betrayal not to act. Doing nothing feels like doing less. The screens flash, the alerts ping, and stillness begins to look like complacency. This is precisely why the boredom edge is real. *It is behaviourally expensive for most people to access.* In a world optimised for hyperactivity, inactivity looks irrational—even when it isn't.

That cognitive dissonance is weaponised by financial intermediaries. Advisory firms, brokerages, and media platforms all operate on engagement economics. "Hold your course" does not generate clicks. "Sell everything now" does. The wealthy—often advised by independent, fee-based fiduciaries—are insulated from this performative cycle. Their boredom is unleveraged. Their capital is not being monetised for attention. As a result, they can sit still *while the rest of the world monetises movement.*

Philosophically, this distinction speaks to a deeper insight: the difference between wealth as entertainment versus wealth as endurance. The former needs novelty; the latter prefers monotony. In the first framework, markets are arenas of action. In the second, they are landscapes to traverse with care. Where the retail investor sees excitement, the strategic allocator sees noise. This is not condescension; it is calibration. *The excitement gap often reveals the experience gap.*

The boredom edge is particularly powerful during periods of macro dislocation. In 2008, during the financial crisis, many HNW investors resisted the urge to sell into panic—not because they had superior forecasts, but because they had designed systems that *disincentivised reaction.* They didn't call their brokers. They didn't log into their dashboards. Their portfolios, dull as they seemed, absorbed the volatility with grace. Similarly, during the COVID crash of March 2020, those with automatic rebalancing protocols or pre-established thresholds acted with discipline. *The pre-commitment to boredom outperformed the temptation of genius.*

It is tempting to believe that financial advantage is driven by brilliance. And in some cases, it is. But in aggregate, the defining characteristic of long-term outperformance is not mental horsepower—it is *behavioural durability.* The ability to stick with a boring plan in the face of novelty, noise, and narrative drift. This is not the kind of insight that makes for flashy TED talks. But it is the kind that survives.

In institutional settings, this edge is formalised. University endowments, for instance, often operate under strategic asset allocations that are reviewed annually, not weekly. The Yale model, pioneered by David Swensen, placed premium value on long-term illiquid positions not just for their returns, but for their behavioural insulation. Endowments do not panic-sell. Their slowness is a feature, not a bug. Their boredom is systemic, not incidental.

Yet the real lesson is psychological, not structural. Anyone can choose slowness. Anyone can resist the itch. But it requires reframing boredom not as a bug, but as *evidence of alignment.* If your investment strategy never bores you, it may not be long-term enough. If your career path never tests your patience, it may be too short-sighted. If your financial plan demands excitement to hold your attention, it may be working against your future self.

The boredom edge is not about suppressing curiosity. It is about recognising where action creates value—and where it merely generates noise. In a world trained to associate movement with progress, choosing stillness is radical. But in the compounding arc of time, it is often the only choice that endures. For those with the courage to tolerate it, boredom is not a tax—it is a dividend in disguise.

Emotional Diversification

In conversations about wealth preservation, most of the attention tends to orbit tangible assets—portfolios, property, trusts, and tax arbitrage. Yet among the truly entrenched wealthy, a subtler form of insurance often proves just as critical: the diversification of emotional exposure. For individuals whose net worth runs into the eight- or nine-figure range, vulnerability rarely stems from financial volatility alone. Instead, risk lives in identity collapse, social demotion, or the psychological weight of perceived failure. These risks may not erode wealth directly, but they destabilise the mental composure required to steward it. To manage this, many affluent individuals diversify not only what they own, but who they are—spreading their self-worth across a deliberately cultivated portfolio of roles, reputations, and relationships.

Emotional diversification, in this context, refers to the strategic allocation of psychological identity across multiple domains to avoid becoming overexposed to the emotional consequences of any single failure. Just as an investor doesn't tie their entire net worth to a single stock, high-net-worth individuals often do not tie their sense of self to a singular professional role, title, or enterprise. The rationale is simple but profound: the more narrowly your identity is tied to any one thing—your company, your investment track record, your status in a specific social hierarchy—the more exposed you are if that thing falters. The wealthy mitigate that exposure not just with financial hedges, but with identity hedges.

One might encounter a venture capitalist who is also a university trustee, a museum board member, a sports team minority owner, and the author of a recently published book. Each of these roles serves a function beyond ego stroking or vanity; they are emotional derivatives, instruments designed to buffer the self from shocks. If a fund underperforms, she is still a public intellectual. If the press turns on her investments, she has cultural capital through the arts. The identity never rests solely on one point of potential failure. *Emotional optionality* is the psychological twin of financial diversification: different identity instruments performing in different macro and micro cycles, ensuring that reputation and confidence remain intact.

Status management is another layer of this equation. Status is not merely a social byproduct of wealth; it is a form of ambient security. For the wealthy, status offers access, insulation, and psychological reinforcement. But maintaining status requires strategic calibration. Individuals in elite circles often manage multiple status anchors simultaneously: legacy, innovation, affiliation, and contribution. Legacy might be expressed through lineage or philanthropy. Innovation through association with tech, biotech, or green capital. Affiliation comes via memberships, clubs, and gated institutions. Contribution is expressed in boards, foundations, and mentorship platforms. The goal is not to dominate all arenas, but to be seen as relevant in several—such that the failure of one does not collapse the edifice.

It's in this context that the truly strategic wealthy demonstrate a paradoxical strength: restraint. They do not pursue constant recognition from a single arena. Instead, they *rotate the centre of gravity of their identity* over time, much like a balanced portfolio reallocates over different market cycles. When their public profile as a financier cools, their voice in academia or culture rises. When a business exits, they shift to policy or education. The movement is not erratic but timed—each identity held lightly enough to avoid emotional overexposure, yet seriously enough to retain social legitimacy.

This approach also offers insulation from crises—personal, professional, or reputational. Consider the HNW executive who retreats from public boards during litigation, not in disgrace but to "focus on climate philanthropy." The narrative is carefully curated, but the structure was prepared in advance. He had already laid the track of emotional diversification before it was needed, giving him the agility to switch roles without collapse. This is not spin; it's *emotional liquidity*. Identity here behaves like an asset class—one with optionality, resilience, and narrative versatility.

Interestingly, emotional diversification is not just about protecting the individual—it also stabilises decision-making. When someone's entire self-image is tied to an asset or enterprise, their risk behaviour becomes distorted. The incentive to double down, deny reality, or panic-sell rises. But when identity is spread across multiple legitimate domains, one can exit an investment or take a reputational hit with less existential threat. The decision becomes economic, not identity-laden. This separation enables clearer judgement, longer time horizons, and more graceful exits. *It is often not money that keeps the wealthy rational under pressure—it is diversified identity.*

This practice begins early for those born into wealth. Private schools, multiple extracurriculars, dual degrees, family foundations, summer internships in art, science, and politics—these are not simply opportunities for skill accumulation. They are scaffolding for a diversified emotional identity. By adulthood, these individuals can pivot between personas depending on context—economist in one room, environmentalist in another, heir in a third. Each persona is authentic, yet none holds absolute power over their sense of self. This flexibility protects against the fragility that plagues those who invest emotionally in a single ladder or metric.

In contrast, many middle-class professionals—especially high-achieving ones—attach identity to one source: profession. Their self-worth rides on performance metrics, job titles, and employer brands. When a job is lost or a promotion missed, the blow is not merely financial; it's existential. This narrow identity allocation makes it harder to rebound, reframe, or reinvent. The wealthy, by contrast, tend to live in a lattice, not a ladder. There is always another rung adjacent, never just above or below.

Philosophically, this speaks to a broader view of the self. Emotional diversification suggests that identity is not fixed but *constructed*, and the most strategically affluent treat that construction like a dynamic asset class. They reinvest, reallocate, and occasionally write off obsolete pieces. They do not view their sense of self as static or sacred, but as an evolving portfolio of roles and relationships that serve larger life outcomes—stability, contribution, adaptability, and control.

This mindset also reveals why many high-net-worth individuals are far less "public" than their means would allow. Silence, obscurity, and opacity are themselves tools of emotional diversification. If one's primary identity is not being a celebrity, public scrutiny carries less emotional risk. The quiet billionaire who operates through proxy foundations and indirect influence is often more psychologically agile than the mogul-turned-influencer whose brand rises and falls with each market cycle.

In times of social volatility—think economic recessions, political unrest, or cultural shifts—this kind of identity pluralism is not a luxury. It is a stabiliser. Those with diversified emotional portfolios tend to adapt better, act more strategically, and suffer fewer permanent hits to their self-concept. They do not need the world to validate a singular identity, because they are not betting their entire emotional balance sheet on it.

Ultimately, the wealth that lasts is stewarded by minds that do not flinch at the chaos of change. That psychological durability is not just born from confidence or intellect, but from insulation—the layered insulation of self-worth built on more than one pillar. In this way, emotional diversification is not soft or secondary. It is foundational. For the wealthy, it's not merely a way of feeling better. It is *how they stay in the game.*

Case Study: The Investor Who Did Nothing and Won

In the financial world, inaction is rarely celebrated. Our modern culture of hyper-responsiveness rewards decisiveness, activity, and the illusion of control. But among the quietly wealthy, a different ethos sometimes prevails—one grounded not in reaction, but in restraint. Nowhere is this more evident than in the story of an ultra-high-net-worth (UHNW) investor whose most lucrative decision was to *do nothing.* Not out of paralysis or ignorance, but from a place of informed stillness and disciplined perspective. His story—anonymous by choice, yet mirrored by a select few—offers a compelling rebuttal to the myth that wealth survives through movement alone.

The investor in question, a third-generation steward of a £400 million family office based in Geneva, has lived through four major financial downturns over three decades. Each time, his advisers, peers, and market commentators issued calls to act: sell tech, rotate sectors, hedge emerging markets, shift into cash. And each time, he listened, absorbed... and declined to act. He made only one move: to rebalance minimally, according to a fixed, rule-based allocation model set in place years prior. No sudden pivots, no contrarian trades, no defensive panic. Just strategic stillness.

This was not the stillness of complacency, but of design. His allocation—roughly 60% global equities, 30% fixed income, and 10% private investments—was engineered for durability, not drama. His process prioritised time horizon over timing, guided by a deeply internalised belief: *volatility is the cost of admission, not a threat to be dodged.* For many, that insight alone would be transformative.

Across the dot-com bust, the 2008 financial crisis, the 2020 pandemic crash, and the 2022 inflation-driven selloff, this "do-nothing" approach resulted in average compounded annual returns of 7.4%, net of fees. Not spectacular, but vastly superior to the post-fact regret of most who sold at the bottom and re-entered too late. More crucially, it preserved both capital and peace of mind—two things the rich are uniquely skilled at protecting in tandem.

What makes this case extraordinary is not the math, but the psychology. Most investors—particularly wealthy ones—experience an inverse relationship between portfolio size and emotional distance. As stakes increase, so too does the temptation to interfere. The myth of mastery whispers ever louder: surely someone with this much capital *must* act when the storm hits. But here, the silence became the edge.

This restraint was not cultivated in a vacuum. It was institutionalised through governance. The family office operated with an investment committee structure that required any portfolio deviation beyond a 5% threshold to be approved by unanimous vote. This forced friction—intentional bureaucracy—acted as a brake on impulsive adjustments. Rather than bottleneck innovation, it filtered out noise-driven decisions.

There's a subtle brilliance in this architecture: the investor outsourced not his judgement, but his *temptation.* The very structure around him was designed to slow him down when adrenaline might otherwise take over. *Slowness as discipline*, not deficiency. In behavioural finance, this is the equivalent of setting up a fail-safe system to outsmart one's future irrational self.

Contrast this with the standard operating mode of many affluent investors during downturns. Fear-driven reallocations, short-termism disguised as tactical brilliance, and decision-making loops that mistake busyness for progress. The UHNW class is often assumed to possess superior information—and many do—but this case shows that information alone is insufficient. *How one interprets and resists that information becomes the differentiator.*

Wealth magnifies fear as much as it does possibility. When losses appear, the pressure to "protect legacy" or "not lose what was built" intensifies. Media coverage of billionaires losing billions within days reinforces the urge to act, to assert control. But as this investor demonstrated, control is often illusion. Risk cannot be removed, only recontextualised.

Doing nothing is not free of cost. It requires tolerating discomfort while everyone else panics, holding one's nerve when social proof vanishes. The headlines scream collapse; the group chats go quiet; the banks grow cautious. And in the centre of it all, the temptation to *just do something* peaks. Yet *this is the crucible in which generational wealth is forged or forfeited.*

Ironically, this investor was not celebrated during the downturns. Within his own advisory circles, he was seen as aloof, overly conservative, even "out of touch with today's tools." Some partners lobbied to adopt more agile, AI-enhanced trading overlays. He declined. Others proposed real-time macro hedging based on geopolitical forecasts. He declined again. Now, years later, many of those proposals are cited as costly distractions that underperformed his unglamorous simplicity.

His children, two of whom are trained in behavioural economics, have since codified his approach into what they call the "Inactivity Premium"—the compound advantage gained not through superior forecasts, but through superior *inaction bias*. It's a term that has quietly circulated among multi-family offices and is now being modelled into a training framework for the next generation.

This concept deserves scrutiny. Most financial education focuses on action verbs: diversify, hedge, rebalance, allocate. But the concept of *deliberate non-action* as a tool of advantage is almost taboo. Especially in a cultural climate that equates ambition with constant motion. Yet, here we see an investor who won not because he anticipated better—but because he *interfered less.*

His model is not replicable for everyone. It requires deep liquidity, low leverage, a high tolerance for paper losses, and institutional-grade governance. But the lesson scales conceptually: *discretion can outperform intervention*, especially when systems are designed to absorb rather than react.

In closing—not in sentiment but in structural insight—this case study reminds us of a broader truth: the wealthy often stay wealthy not because they know more, but because they *disturb less.* They engineer systems that respect time, respect risk, and respect silence. Sometimes, the greatest financial move is to make none at all.

Chapter 9
The Code of Quiet Wealth

In the architecture of lasting wealth, silence often speaks louder than status. While conspicuous consumption grabs headlines and fuels envy, those who endure across generations tend to operate on a subtler frequency—one attuned not to applause, but to insulation. Experience teaches that visibility carries risk: exposure invites scrutiny, litigation, regulatory attention, and social expectation. Discretion, conversely, offers layers of protection—legal, social, and psychological. Among dynastic families, quiet is not mere preference; it is a deliberate, often intergenerational strategy of risk management.

At first glance, such opacity may appear aloof or passive. In reality, it is strategic. Across European landholding dynasties and American financial lineages alike, a shared principle prevails: the longer capital must endure, the less noise it can afford. This insight manifests in trusts, legal shields, family constitutions, and offshore structures—but also in subtler behavioural codes: how one speaks, travels, dresses, and publicly endorses—or withholds endorsement.

Transitioning from accumulation to preservation triggers a psychological inversion. Ambition yields to discretion—not retreat, but recalibration. In a world where wealth can be weaponised politically, socially, or legally, the goal becomes to vanish from the limelight without leaving the stage. Ultra-high-net-worth families frequently eschew media profiles or named philanthropic initiatives, not from modesty, but from an understanding that scrutiny often scales faster than prestige. Registering jets or yachts through offshore entities is rarely about tax evasion; it is about shielding operational visibility from journalists, activists, and adversaries.

Among legal advisers, the term "reputational firewall" captures the layered approach used to segment exposure: ownership is obscured, association delayed, identities distributed across jurisdictions. Yet the subtler firewall is behavioural. The cultivated art of being underestimated—projecting moderation, downplaying status, appearing benign—deflects inquiry, reduces perceived threat, and creates breathing space.

Consider the patriarch driving a decade-old Volvo despite controlling a multi-billion-dollar property portfolio, or an heiress who speaks modestly about "helping with family matters" rather than managing a global luxury brand's strategy arm. These choices are deliberate. In elite circles, the highest compliment is to pass unnoticed. This ethos extends to private investment clubs and social calendars centred on discreet salons rather than televised galas: influence is inversely proportional to projection.

Such restraint is not weakness. Indeed, it is soft power at full intensity. Wealth expressed loudly burns bright but fleeting; wealth wielded quietly embeds deeply and endures. From quietly endowed university chairs to behind-the-scenes political advisory roles, durable influence is often institutional rather than personal. Names rarely appear on press releases, yet impact is felt in legislation, cultural endowments, and multigenerational strategy. Influence is designed, not flaunted.

The advantages of discretion become especially apparent during turbulence. In the 2008 financial crisis, publicly visible families were frequent targets of populist ire. Those who maintained low profiles, operating through generic family offices or holding companies, navigated the storm with fewer reputational bruises. Visibility is liability in volatile times. Many influential financiers operate without social media, public statements, or press appearances, yet orchestrate billions in capital flow.

Quiet does not imply disengagement. On the contrary, these individuals shape public life via proxies—lobbying arms, think tanks, universities, curated philanthropy. Their fingerprints are present in policy direction, board appointments, and academic discourse, even if their names never appear publicly. They are architects of the background.

This ethos extends into family culture. Children of quietly wealthy families are often raised with an intentional absence of flamboyance—not solely for humility, but to reduce exposure, risk, and entitlement. In elite schools, an unspoken hierarchy distinguishes those who flaunt wealth from those who master concealment. The latter are groomed for custodianship. In some families, heirs learn the full scope of assets only in their late twenties or later—creating insulation from early distortion and allowing identity formation before asset awareness.

Some critics may argue that this culture deprives society of aspirational role models or democratic visibility. From the perspective of capital preservation, the question is not inspiration, but endurance. In an age of pervasive data, AI profiling, and click-driven outrage, durability demands strategic ambiguity.

Ironically, the most enduring capital often escapes notice. Forbes lists, Instagram mansions, and high-profile IPOs highlight ephemeral visibility. Beneath the surface lie dynasties whose names remain unknown, whose holdings are invisible to the public eye, whose influence flows through intermediaries rather than interviews. Their power compounds not through display, but through intentional quiet.

This chapter reveals an ethos counter to modern social norms: influence grows with silence, power operates invisibly yet decisively, and wealth designed to last seeks shelter in shadow rather than status. This is not a story of the loud and celebrated. It is the anatomy of discretion as strategy, camouflage as capital, and restraint as inheritance. Silence, here, is deliberate, engineered, and profoundly effective.

Visibility as Vulnerability

Wealth confers power, but it also attracts attention—some of it corrosive, some of it criminal. In the realm of enduring wealth, visibility is rarely a neutral state. To be seen too clearly is to be targeted—by litigants, regulators, blackmailers, opportunists, even one's own social peers. That is why, contrary to popular portrayals, many of the wealthiest families and individuals do not seek visibility but actively design their lives around its avoidance. Discretion is not a matter of modesty. It is a strategic defence mechanism—legal, reputational, and psychological—intended to safeguard the compound advantages that capital requires to endure.

What the wealthy understand, often through hard-won experience, is that exposure multiplies risk faster than it generates reward. For those already in possession of considerable assets, the marginal benefit of recognition or status signalling is usually outweighed by the legal liabilities, media scrutiny, and social resentment that can accompany it. This logic—rarely spoken, always practised—forms a quiet doctrine among multigenerational wealth: privacy is not a luxury. It is a moat.

Consider the legal dimension. The structure of wealth ownership among ultra-high-net-worth (UHNW) families is almost always obfuscated for a reason. Assets are not held directly but through cascading layers of trusts, foundations, holding companies, and offshore structures—not purely for tax efficiency, but to render the asset map illegible to outsiders. When assets are difficult to trace, they are harder to sue for, harder to seize, harder to scandalise. Litigation risk is not hypothetical at the highest levels of wealth—it is ambient and constant. As one elite wealth attorney once remarked, "If your name is in the registry, you've already made a mistake."

Beyond legal risk lies the reputational layer. Visibility invites judgement, particularly in a cultural climate where affluence is increasingly associated with excess or moral failing. The rise of public scrutiny—fuelled by social media, activist journalism, and populist sentiment—means that visible wealth becomes performative, even provocative. Families that understand this dynamic do not retreat into paranoia; they adopt what might be called *preemptive modesty*. They downplay lifestyle displays. They under-communicate success. They hire PR strategists not to promote but to deflect. In elite circles, *the truly rich often appear poorer than they are—by choice, not necessity.*

Psychologically, too, discretion offers insulation. Visibility distorts interpersonal dynamics—skewing relationships toward transactionality, fuelling envy, eroding trust. It is hard to be seen for one's character when one's balance sheet precedes the conversation. Thus, those who have lived for decades in wealthy enclaves often develop *a preference for normalcy not out of ascetic virtue but as a hedge against disconnection.* This is especially true in families that seek to transmit wealth across generations. Inheritance is not just the transfer of capital; it is the transfer of identity. And if children are raised in an environment where visibility equals validation, they are more likely to squander not just assets but integrity.

There is an instructive contrast between "loud money" and "quiet money." Loud money announces itself through media profiles, magazine covers, and highly publicised donations. It seeks visibility as a proxy for impact. Quiet money, by contrast, seeks influence without spectacle. It funds endowments, builds institutions, supports policy initiatives—but does so through intermediaries, proxies, or silent partnerships. It is no less ambitious. But it recognises that *power flows longer when it flows invisibly.*

Some of the most powerful dynastic families in finance, philanthropy, and politics operate under this principle. Their names rarely appear in the press—not because they are irrelevant, but because they are structurally absent from the surface. They have mastered the art of *staying behind the veil,* influencing outcomes without attracting attention. They pay premiums for anonymity—using intermediaries to buy property, working through family offices instead of personal accounts, operating with legal structures that decouple ownership from attribution. Their PR strategy is omission. Their risk mitigation is obscurity.

This is not to suggest that visibility is inherently bad, only that it comes at a cost—and that cost rises in proportion to wealth. For entrepreneurs and public figures, visibility can be instrumental—building a brand, attracting capital, establishing authority. But for those whose wealth is already entrenched, *the calculus flips.* Publicity becomes a liability. And the most astute stewards of capital behave accordingly.

The behavioural implications are subtle but systematic. Wealthy individuals do not just hide what they own—they learn to *behave inconspicuously.* They avoid provocative clothing, steer clear of political commentary, and rarely speak publicly about their net worth. Their children are taught to blend in, not stand out. They attend elite schools, but not the flashiest ones. They invest in art, but often lend it anonymously. Their digital footprints are minimised. Their social media accounts—if they exist—are bland or locked. These behaviours are not accidental. They are *tactics in a larger architecture of invisibility*.

Even in philanthropy, discretion often governs approach. While some use donations to buy name recognition, many wealthy families prefer donor-advised funds or anonymous endowments. Their influence may extend across education, healthcare, and policy—but the public trail ends with an institution, not a surname. This anonymity is not apathy. It is a form of strategic restraint—a desire to shape the world without becoming its spectacle.

Crisis events amplify the logic of discretion. During economic crashes, political upheavals, or regime changes, visible wealth is often the first to be targeted. Whether through taxation, seizure, or reputational attack, the exposed are made examples of. In contrast, families that have invested in discretion often ride out these storms with minimal damage—not because they are morally superior, but because *they are structurally less visible*. Their interests are less traceable, their vulnerabilities less exploitable.

The lesson here is neither paranoia nor concealment for its own sake. Rather, it is the recognition that *sustainable wealth management is as much about behavioural design as financial strategy*. Visibility is not a neutral by-product of success. It is a variable to be managed—actively, thoughtfully, and with clear awareness of its second-order consequences.

There is also a generational dimension. Wealth earned through entrepreneurial hustle often begins in visibility—media profiles, keynote speeches, status symbols. But if that wealth matures into legacy, the strategy often shifts toward discretion. The second generation becomes less vocal, the third less public still. *Enduring wealth behaves differently from emergent wealth*. It speaks softly, acts slowly, and prioritises stability over spectacle.

Even the language of wealth shifts with this sensibility. Families that prioritise discretion tend to use terms like "stewardship" instead of "success," "legacy" instead of "lifestyle," "governance" instead of "control." These are not semantic flourishes—they reflect an underlying philosophy: *to remain powerful, one must not always appear powerful.*

In a world increasingly obsessed with visibility—where likes, clicks, and public status drive behaviour—this restraint might seem anachronistic. But in elite financial circles, *invisibility is the new status signal.* Not because it hides weakness, but because it reveals confidence. Those who no longer need to be seen are often the ones who have already won. And those who stay unseen tend to stay secure.

Ultimately, the doctrine of quiet wealth is not about hiding from the world. It is about *building structures that outlast public moods.* It is about owning without shouting, influencing without imprinting, moving without trace. It is not a conspiracy of the rich. It is simply *a more durable way to inhabit privilege.* And for those who understand its logic, visibility is not proof of power. It is often the beginning of its erosion.

The Art of Being Underestimated

Power, when effectively wielded, often hides in plain sight. The most formidable influence is frequently cloaked in modesty, not magnified by spectacle. Across centuries and civilisations, individuals and families who have managed to stay rich—and stay in control—have learned a timeless lesson: *being underestimated is not a liability; it is an asset.* In the intricate architecture of quiet wealth, underexposure is not incidental but intentional. To the truly strategic, modesty is a form of insulation. It dampens threat, reduces competition, and affords manoeuvrability. The capacity to influence events while escaping scrutiny is, for many, a far more potent privilege than open dominance.

For the ultra-wealthy, particularly those embedded in dynastic wealth or discreet private capital, invisibility is not merely a lifestyle choice—it is a safeguard. In a global culture addicted to visibility, with algorithms amplifying noise and status markers becoming commodified, remaining unremarkable by design is an uncommon discipline. What seems like humility may, in practice, be calculated under-projection. In place of the performative gestures that mark nouveau-riche confidence—luxury branding, viral philanthropy, or media-facing success—old money often leans on ambiguity, misdirection, or aesthetic restraint to shield power from visibility. Where others chase the perception of wealth, the quietly powerful concern themselves with its preservation.

The mechanisms of being underestimated are psychological as much as strategic. One learns not only how to play small, but how to *look* small to those watching. This involves linguistic discipline, visual choices, and the cultivation of an unthreatening narrative. The language is never that of domination, but of stewardship. The appearance is not of hunger, but of heritage. Wealth is signalled, if at all, through contextual fluency, not ornamentation—through the subtle codes of familiarity with place, institution, or tradition. A low-key Oxford accent, a weathered cashmere jumper, or a well-worn Saab parked among Range Rovers may say more than any Rolex ever could. *The more important the fortune, the quieter the symbols.*

Importantly, this modesty is not passive. It is engineered. The structures around wealthy families—legal trusts, private family offices, PR consultants, estate managers—are designed to reinforce an ecosystem of understatement. They do not only manage assets, but narrative. The right tax structure can obscure beneficial ownership; the right foundation can absorb reputational shocks; the right gatekeeper can make even public-facing engagements feel opaque. Consider the role of a discreet legal firm, whose services ensure both regulatory compliance and image containment. Or a communications advisor whose sole task is to keep the client's name out of stories—not in them.

Case in point: the Rothschilds. Despite being among the most powerful financial families in modern history, their public profiles remain deliberately blurred. No overexposure. No performative capitalism. Their institutions operate quietly, their philanthropic arms focus on durable legacy, and their capital speaks only when needed. A similar ethos permeates more contemporary holdings. In Silicon Valley, one finds a growing counter-current to the loud, self-aggrandising founder culture. The most enduring investors—those whose positions outlast cycles—are often the least known. Not because they lack vision, but because their power is protected by discretion.

The underestimated rarely need to posture. Because they know something the overexposed often forget: *the need to appear powerful is inversely correlated with actual influence.* Those who move billions do not need to announce it. They may appear at conferences as moderators, not keynote speakers. They may invest through proxies, not headline-grabbing vehicles. Their decision-making rooms are smaller, quieter, and more insulated from the pressures of perception. Their social media presence is either absent or deliberately muted. Their victories, when visible at all, are narrated by others.

There is also an institutional advantage in projecting modesty. The understated do not attract aggressive regulation, media antagonism, or activist scrutiny in the same way high-profile billionaires do. A name that never trends online is a name unlikely to be subpoenaed out of political convenience. Discretion affords time, room for error, and insulation from the volatility of public sentiment. In moments of market stress, those who stayed out of sight often remain out of blame. This is no accident. It is a choice made decades prior, when the family first declined the high-profile investment award or refused to list their company for media glory.

Psychologically, being underestimated permits a broader strategic range. It allows a form of arbitrage. Competitors misjudge capacity; regulators under-prioritise oversight; even peers may misallocate credit. This misalignment creates space. Consider the family office that quietly acquires farmland, not as an ESG performance gesture, but as a long-term geopolitical hedge. Or the low-profile investor who funds policy institutes and university chairs, not for ego, but to shape the philosophical frameworks of future lawmakers. These are not gestures of status—they are blueprints for influence. *Influence sustained over time needs cover, not spotlight.*

The art of being underestimated does not imply a disavowal of ambition. On the contrary, it is the shape that long-term ambition takes when paired with prudence. The underestimated often work on decade timelines, not quarterly ones. Their patience is not lethargy, but design. They understand that credibility compounds faster when unencumbered by vanity. By skipping the performance of dominance, they preserve optionality. They can pivot, reallocate, absorb shocks—without having to narrate their every move.

In environments where signalling drives behaviour—especially among newer capital or status-chasing classes—there is immense competitive advantage in not playing the game at all. While others react to media cycles, chase visibility metrics, or craft personal brands, the underestimated build capacity in silence. They take counsel, not applause. They watch markets, not followers. And when the dust settles, they are often the ones holding durable assets, not reputational liabilities.

There is, too, a moral complexity to this posture. It creates tension. Some view this form of self-concealment as manipulative or elitist. And occasionally, it is. But that critique misses the more central point: *underestimation is not always deception; it is often protection.* Protection from envy. Protection from shallow scrutiny. Protection from the fragility that comes when one's financial persona is more valuable than the underlying wealth itself. And most of all, protection for the next generation, who can inherit not only assets, but anonymity.

As economic cycles sharpen and political winds shift, the underestimated may be the last ones standing. Not because they were the smartest, loudest, or most ambitious—but because they chose discretion over display, continuity over theatrics, and power over performance. They knew, before others did, that *invisibility isn't weakness—it is resilience in its purest form.*

Soft Power, Quiet Influence

The wealthiest individuals in society rarely seek applause; they seek advantage. Not the kind that demands attention, but the kind that endures—compounded not in headlines, but in policy papers, charitable boards, and quiet conversations at institutions the public rarely sees up close. While mass culture tends to associate power with visibility—political charisma, corporate dominance, ostentatious lifestyle—the most enduring form of power is neither shouted nor staged. It is arranged, sustained, and, critically, *designed to appear unremarkable.*

Wealth, at a certain level, becomes less about consumption and more about insulation. The truly rich—those for whom wealth has transitioned from personal achievement to generational infrastructure—are acutely aware that visibility courts volatility. They've learned that loud money may dominate a moment, but quiet money shapes decades. One of the least acknowledged pillars of this quiet influence is *soft power*—a term more often applied to geopolitics, yet increasingly relevant when observing the behavioural strategies of high-net-worth individuals (HNWIs) and families. At this level, capital is not just a medium of exchange; it's a medium of persuasion.

Soft power manifests in three principal domains: philanthropy, policy access, and institutional integration. Each is a subtle but potent tool, designed not for control in the hard sense—through coercion or force—but for steering outcomes over time. It is about shaping the terrain rather than dictating the path, about altering what's normal, viable, or desirable. And the wealthy have mastered this slow, deliberate shaping better than any other class.

Philanthropy, for instance, is often assumed to be an act of generosity, when in fact it frequently serves as an instrument of ideology. The donation of capital to educational initiatives, medical research, or public policy think tanks may seem purely altruistic. But beneath this surface lies a pattern: philanthropic capital directs intellectual traffic. A foundation endows a university chair not merely to foster research but to nudge the centre of gravity in a particular intellectual direction. A major gift to a medical institution might prioritise research into diseases that disproportionately affect donors' communities—or, more subtly, position a family name inside the heart of respected civic life. The reward is not publicity, but permanency. *The philanthropic donor does not need to dominate headlines to dominate the agenda.*

This soft power has structural efficiency. Tax structures in many jurisdictions reward philanthropic giving, making it not only reputationally virtuous but economically rational. But the strategic return on this giving is more psychological than financial. When a wealthy individual gives large sums to a prestigious institution, they are purchasing a kind of narrative immunity—a public record of benevolence that can cushion future scrutiny or controversy. Philanthropy offers an image of moral clarity that transcends balance sheets and portfolios. It is a reputational hedge.

Policy influence is even more discreet. Whereas lobbying is explicit and often regulated, the wealthiest individuals tend to operate through more rarefied channels—think advisory panels, strategic donations to political action committees, or invitation-only events where public policy and private wealth quietly intersect. The distinction is critical. While lobbying is transactional—"support this bill and receive X"—the soft power elite engage in long-term relational capital building. They underwrite white papers, host legislators at forums, and build rapport with key figures over years, not weeks. The return on investment is not in a single policy shift but in access itself—the ability to inject perspective before decisions are finalised.

This is not inherently sinister. In some cases, it ensures the voices of capital-intensive sectors—healthcare innovation, green technology, infrastructure—are factored into policymaking. But the asymmetry is clear: most citizens vote; a few *shape what's up for a vote to begin with.* Power at this level is not exercised through confrontation, but calibration. And the most successful actors ensure their hands remain invisible.

The third channel—institutions—is perhaps the least understood and most underestimated. This includes not just formal positions on boards or endowments, but also informal networks: alumni circles, family office syndicates, research grants, cultural foundations. These are the places where future leaders are vetted, future narratives are sculpted, and elite consensus is cultivated. In this ecosystem, wealthy individuals are not simply members—they are architects. They influence who gets platformed, which problems are prioritised, and what kinds of solutions are deemed respectable.

This long view requires patience. Unlike venture capital, where returns are benchmarked quarterly, soft power is compounding influence. It rewards consistency and reputational depth. Wealthy individuals understand that capital moves markets, but *credibility moves systems.* And the route to credibility is not through domination but affiliation—by being seen as a steward, not a manipulator.

Yet this quiet architecture is not without contradiction. The very institutions that provide soft power are also under growing scrutiny. Questions about how philanthropic gifts influence academic research, how donor-funded think tanks shape public policy, and how elite access affects democracy are increasingly pointed. In response, many wealthy families are refining their strategies—not abandoning soft power, but doubling down on discretion. They are professionalising foundation governance, distancing themselves publicly from political action, and seeking roles that confer *influence without ownership.*

For instance, a family might fund a journalism fellowship focused on investigative reporting into public corruption—a virtuous initiative on its face, but one that also earns the donor credibility as a guardian of democracy. Simultaneously, the same family might own infrastructure assets that benefit from the same policy conversations shaped by that journalism. The two threads never officially meet—but they do, subtly, shape a coherent influence ecosystem. *Power is more persuasive when it wears the mask of principle.*

The behavioural logic here is consistent: wealth that endures is not concerned with being liked, but with being listened to. And influence that's designed to be quiet often travels further than the kind that demands attention. This has profound implications for how we understand social mobility and class dynamics. It suggests that access is not just about income or even net worth—but about ideological footprint. Who gets to shape the terms of public discourse? Whose views become the default assumptions of experts and policymakers? Quiet wealth ensures that its voice precedes its identity—ideas are seeded before anyone asks who paid for them.

Perhaps the most important feature of soft power is that it's resilient. Market shocks may erode capital, scandals may taint legacy names, but institutions remember their benefactors. A building named after a donor will survive a decade's worth of criticism. A funded research agenda can outlive a CEO's tenure. *Reputation, when deeply embedded, has a longer shelf life than liquidity.*

Understanding this dynamic doesn't require cynicism. It requires clarity. The enduring wealthy are not simply rich in assets—they are rich in *narrative control.* They influence what is considered good, normal, and important. Their soft power is not accidental—it is strategic, sophisticated, and often invisible until its effects are fully in place.

To ignore this form of influence is to misunderstand how modern power works. To study it is not to resent it, but to recognise that money alone does not determine who shapes the world. *It is the architecture around the money—the reputation, relationships, and restraint—that quietly steers the levers of legacy.* And for those building wealth not merely to enjoy, but to preserve, this soft power is not optional. It is foundational.

How Not to Signal Wealth

At the upper echelons of enduring wealth, the question is not how much one owns, but how little one appears to need. In a world increasingly obsessed with signalling—likes, follows, valuations—the truly wealthy often move in the opposite direction, towards opacity. Not because they are modest by temperament, but because *discretion is structural.* Visibility carries a cost: in scrutiny, in expectation, in vulnerability. The rich who stay rich learn early that the loudest wealth is often the shortest-lived. To endure, they master a subtler discipline: the art of not looking rich.

Wealth signalling is no longer just about luxury. In a hyperconnected economy where public perception shapes everything from legal risk to political exposure, displaying affluence is no longer merely crass—it is strategically unwise. This is not a new insight. For centuries, old money families have curated appearances that divert attention, deflect envy, and disarm adversaries. What has changed is the sophistication of these cues, and the degree to which they are now understood as strategic tools—conscious acts of camouflage in a society trained to see status through consumption.

Consider clothing. While aspirational classes often associate wealth with logo-saturated luxury, those with enduring capital know that *the more overt the label, the newer the money*. The rich wear quality, not branding. The tailoring is precise, the fabrics exceptional, the design timeless—but the brand is usually unreadable unless you are part of the same social tier. Italian cashmere with no emblem will always outsignal a monogrammed hoodie, to those who matter. Here, value is not demonstrated through identification, but through insulation—*the ability to opt out of fashion's seasonal churn without appearing indifferent.*

This extends to cars, watches, homes. A McLaren screams. A well-maintained Land Cruiser whispers. A minimalist Patek Philippe speaks only to those who know where to look. The wealthy choose tools that serve them, not symbols that define them. A high-end residence may sit behind hedges instead of gates, designed not to impress from the curb but to disappear entirely. They invest in privacy architecture: off-market transactions, trust ownership, shell LLCs. These are not tools of evasion but instruments of discretion. *Their wealth is structured not for display, but for durability.*

Yet the most instructive markers are behavioural, not material. One of the clearest tells of deep wealth is the absence of urgency. The wealthy do not rush—not through doors, not through conversations, not through decision-making. They speak less in volume and more in silence. They ask more questions than they answer. They make eye contact but rarely attempt to dominate a room. They rarely need to. Influence, at this level, is understood as *what remains when one leaves the room.* Status signalling becomes inverse: the more you need to demonstrate, the less you possess.

There is also a deliberate downplaying of association. Enduringly wealthy individuals often omit context in introductions. They do not announce what they own, control, or lead. In meetings, they let others speak first. In public, they allow others to occupy attention. This restraint is not passivity—it is asset protection. It allows room for manoeuvre, reduces friction, and creates interpretive ambiguity. *Power that's underestimated is harder to oppose.*

Another subtle tactic is *cultural blending*. Rather than set themselves apart, the wealthy often mirror the habits of their environment—especially in cosmopolitan or meritocratic settings. A billionaire venture capitalist may favour jeans and Allbirds at a board meeting not to appear relatable, but to dissolve into context. The goal is not to be invisible, but *strategically unmemorable*. Their power is felt, not flaunted.

This phenomenon also plays out in language. The wealthy do not broadcast ambition. They rarely talk about "hustle", "scale", or "winning". Those are survival words from earlier stages. Instead, they speak in terms of *risk, exposure, optionality*. Their goals are framed as protection rather than conquest. They talk about legacy, not lifestyle. Liquidity, not leverage. By reversing the aspirational lexicon, they place themselves in a different mental class—one that thinks in terms of stewardship, not statement.

Their social media, if it exists, is curated with an algorithmic precision: family, nature, philanthropy, perhaps a discreet nod to institutional ties. No private jets, no extravagant dinners, no political tirades. The goal is not personal branding. It's *reputational insulation*. Many deploy ghost accounts for real social activity. Visibility is not something they crave—it's something they manage, with discipline.

Even failure is disguised. The enduringly wealthy take reputational losses in private. Business setbacks are cordoned off through legal firewalls or delegated to family offices. Their names remain unsullied even when portfolios collapse. When the public sees a name again, it is usually in the context of restoration, not reckoning. This invisibility during turmoil is not accidental—it is the result of a cultivated life infrastructure designed to *absorb volatility without public consequence*.

Contrast this with performative wealth—the kind often found on social media, where status is monetised through visibility. The more you reveal, the more your audience grows. But this visibility is a double-edged sword. It draws in attention, yes—but also obligation, regulation, and the possibility of scandal. Performative wealth lives on public favour. Quiet wealth lives on *structural distance*. The former is shaped by followers; the latter by foundations.

Yet one must ask: is this invisibility a moral virtue or merely a defensive strategy? The answer lies in the intent. Some choose quiet wealth as a shield—protecting family, legacy, and mental space from the volatility of public life. Others choose it as a veil—obscuring extractive practices or pre-empting social accountability. The behavioural symmetry may be identical, but the ethical terrain differs. *Not signalling wealth does not mean not having responsibility for it.*

It is also worth noting that discretion is a learned art. Many wealthy individuals only embrace invisibility after experiencing its absence. A period of high exposure—whether through business success, social ascent, or youthful exuberance—often precedes the decision to retreat. Publicity becomes a liability; transparency, a tax. This transition from performative to protective is rarely spoken about publicly. But it marks a shift in mindset: from achievement to preservation.

In a world obsessed with metrics and appearance, choosing *not* to display wealth is increasingly countercultural. It requires discipline, strategy, and a willingness to *opt out of applause.* And for those who understand the fragility of reputation, the risks of social volatility, and the permanence of digital footprints, this choice becomes not just a preference but a philosophy. A philosophy where the truest expression of wealth is not what you own, but what you *no longer need to prove.*

The code of quiet wealth, then, is not merely a behavioural checklist—it is a psychological architecture. It reflects a worldview where power is not about presence but *permanence*, where the game is not status but endurance. And in that game, *not signalling wealth* becomes the ultimate move: the one that secures influence, protects capital, and ensures that those who know, know—and those who don't, *never need to.*

Chapter 10
Building Your Own Insulation

Enduring wealth, at its core, is less a matter of possession than of protection. Not the superficial kind that relies on security guards or insurance policies, but structural protection: the capacity to absorb shocks without faltering, to withstand volatility without visibility, to maintain optionality while the world grows more extractive. True, lasting wealth is a product of insulation—the extent to which one's financial and psychological life is buffered from noise, manipulation, and fragility. Where most focus on accumulation, the wise prioritise fortification.

A common misconception is equating insulation with extravagance: fortress homes, offshore trusts, armies of lawyers. Yet the enduring reality is that insulation is defined more by architecture than scale. It is the design of thought, structure, and behaviour. And, crucially, it is accessible long before fortune arrives. This chapter does not seek to replicate the trappings of the affluent; it seeks to uncover their framework. How do some financial lives withstand crises while others crumble? What can be emulated—not in consumption, but in configuration?

Begin with stress. Most financial plans—if they exist—are optimism-oriented, assuming continuity, market growth, institutional reliability. Few are designed for discontinuity: income loss, asset illiquidity, credit contraction, divorce, litigation. The truly enduring think in failure modes. They anticipate vulnerabilities, run scenarios that appear improbable to outsiders, and begin with an uncomfortable honesty: what if my income halved for two years? What if my primary asset froze? What if my partner died tomorrow—would my legal and financial scaffolding serve or strangle me? Stress-testing is prudence, not paranoia; it starts not with spreadsheets, but with confronting fragility.

This mindset is often institutionalised in generational wealth. Family offices run simulations, not forecasts. Liquidity is sacrosanct. Equity exposure is calibrated to survivability, not thrill. Complexity is tolerated only when counterparty risk is understood. The average investor measures growth; the sophisticated investor measures margin for error. Yet these principles are not reserved for billionaires. A personal audit—identifying fragility, entanglements, overexposure—can begin the journey toward insulation. Often, the first step is subtraction: what can fail without unravelling everything?

Equally potent is the behavioural scaffolding. Compartmentalisation, for instance, is as important as financial engineering. Wealthy families create firewalls across identities, not merely entities. Business is not self; investment is not ego. Losses are contained. Anyone can emulate this: maintain diverse income streams, separate spending from earning, establish mental buffers between market swings and self-worth. The richest resilience resides internally.

Legal simplicity, too, is underrated. Effective insulation rarely requires exotic jurisdictions or extraordinary legal teams. Often, it is mundane: consistent use of limited liability structures, basic umbrella insurance, clear wills, living trusts, prenuptial agreements. These are not exclusive to the wealthy—they are available to those who perceive risk not as moral failure, but statistical inevitability. Yet adoption remains sparse, largely because structural thinking about fragility is seldom taught. Early action matters more than scale.

Mental models matter just as much. Perhaps the most powerful is the dual-temporal lens: thinking in decades, acting in seasons. Wealth is built across generations, yet managed with seasonal granularity. Allocations are planned in generational terms, yet spending, liquidity, and exposure are reviewed quarterly. Most act with long-term ambition but short-term panic, oscillating in response to noise. Insulation is coherence over time: zooming out without losing clarity, zooming in without losing perspective.

This mentality shapes everything: career choices become ecosystems of leverage, relationships shift from emotional bonds to resilience multipliers. The insulated life is minimalistic, not in aesthetics, but in friction—wealth at rest, options held lightly, status de-emphasised. The less identity is tied to volatility, the more freedom one retains under pressure.

Perhaps the most counterintuitive insight is the redefinition of wealth itself. Most chase visibility: net worth, accolades, followers. Yet visibility increases fragility, attracting envy, regulators, litigation. The truly powerful retreat into invisible wealth: quiet control, private equity, unleveraged land, minority stakes with veto rights. This wealth is not absent; it is shielded. It moves slowly, outlasts trends, and signals meaning only to those who understand its architecture.

The same principle scales down. A debt-free home, low-cost lifestyle, legal entity protecting creative income—these are forms of insulation. They reduce fragility while preserving agency. Step away from signalling wealth, and time horizons expand. Downturns cease to terrify; one becomes ungovernable by panic.

This chapter provides a blueprint. It does not romanticise the elite, nor urge imitation of their surface. It isolates what is transferable: structural calm, behavioural rigor, mental frameworks, legal simplicity. Wealth is what you can afford not to fear. The fundamental question becomes: what am I building that endures even when all visible assets vanish?

The path to insulation is not gated. It is available to anyone willing to forego status theatre in favour of structural clarity. Money may accelerate the journey, but it does not define the destination. That is determined by the sobriety of habits, the clarity of frameworks, and the courage to build quietly while the world performs loudly.

Stress-Test Your Financial Position

Wealth rarely collapses from a single dramatic blow. It unravels through friction, oversight, and unseen exposure—slowly at first, then suddenly. What breaks people financially isn't necessarily a market crash or a job loss; it's a cascade: the failed assumption that the next paycheque arrives on time, that the interest rate remains stable, that leverage can be refinanced. *Resilience is not built on predicting the future. It is built on preparing for the parts of the future that don't cooperate.* And that preparation begins with a hard question too few ask until it's too late: How fragile is your financial life?

To stress-test your financial position is to behave like an engineer facing load uncertainty, not a gambler chasing return. You are not trying to guess which scenario will unfold—you are interrogating what breaks you, regardless of how likely or unlikely it seems today. This is not budgeting. It is not net worth tracking. It is scenario simulation—systematically identifying where your financial architecture lacks redundancy, flexibility, or endurance. It is the difference between measuring wealth and understanding *what can be lost without losing control.*

Start with liquidity. It is the most misread variable in personal finance. Many associate liquidity with income. But income is not liquidity—it is a claim on a future promise. The critical question is: *how many months could you operate your life, without degradation, if all active income stopped tomorrow?* If your number is less than six, you are vulnerable. If it is under three, you are exposed. If it is under one, you are in a false state of stability—like a high-rise on stilts during calm weather.

But liquidity is not just about bank balances. It's about liquidity of assets, liquidity of access, and liquidity of mind. Ask: Which of your assets can be converted without a haircut? How quickly? Under what market conditions? Is your emergency fund in cash or an ETF? Is it in your own name, or a shared account? Is it parked in an institution that might gate withdrawals in a crisis? *Stress-testing means assuming a scenario where selling is hard and cash is king.* That means understanding the distinction between notional wealth and deployable reserves.

Next, examine concentration. Not just asset concentration, but *income concentration, counterparty concentration, location concentration.* Most people are far more concentrated than they realise. A single employer supplies both salary and healthcare. A mortgage and a spouse are tied to one city. A career trajectory hinges on one industry's health. The question is not whether you are diversified—it's whether you could absorb a correlated shock across these domains. *Concentration is efficient in growth, but lethal in failure.* If your equity, income, and identity are all tied to the same system, your exposure is higher than any spreadsheet reflects.

Now test cost rigidity. Most expenses are not as variable as people imagine. Mortgage payments, school fees, medical plans, minimum loan obligations—these are fixed not just financially, but socially. Cutting them has reputational cost, familial cost, psychological cost. Ask: Which expenses could I reduce by 30% without shame or damage? Which obligations are locked in by lifestyle signaling or dependency? Are there parts of my spending that I mentally classify as "essential" but are, in reality, choices tied to habit or image? *Resilience often lives in the freedom to reduce friction without social erosion.* That freedom is eroded long before a bank balance hits zero.

Debt deserves a separate layer of interrogation. Not all debt is equal—but most people treat it as such. There's a vast difference between a mortgage backed by appreciating equity, and consumer debt backed by nothing but hope. But even "good" debt becomes fragile under duration mismatch. If your repayment terms are misaligned with your income volatility, you are structurally brittle. Ask: Can I service this debt through passive means? Would my repayment ability survive a 40% income cut for two years? If not, am I compensating with arrogance or a belief in smooth outcomes?

Another overlooked test: tax timing. Many self-employed or high-income individuals carry large deferred tax obligations without treating them as liabilities. But taxes aren't optional—they're just late. Treating tax liabilities as a future problem is equivalent to pretending a ballooning credit card balance is invisible because the statement hasn't arrived. *A resilient balance sheet accounts for taxes in real-time—not in fantasy.* If your savings include a silent tax bomb, you are richer on paper than in truth.

Then consider legal and structural fragility. How are your assets held? Are you exposed to litigation risk through business entanglements, co-ownership, or ambiguous contracts? Do you own your primary asset personally, jointly, or via a protective entity? If your income is dependent on IP or personal brand, is it protected by enforceable agreements? Most people ignore structure until it becomes the cause of stress, not the shield against it. The wealthy often invest disproportionately in legal insulation not out of paranoia, but because they understand that *wealth is not just about possession—it is about control under duress.*

Stress-testing also requires examining emotional exposure. What part of your self-worth is tied to money? What happens to your decision-making clarity when markets fall 30%? If your identity is entangled with financial performance, you will amplify downturns with bad decisions—panic selling, pride-based holding, overcompensating. The psychologically insulated can see volatility as data. The emotionally overleveraged see it as threat. *True resilience blends numerical buffers with emotional distance from the numbers themselves.*

To make this actionable, map out scenarios—not forecasts. Forecasts imply probability; scenarios reveal consequences. What happens if the market drops 40% and takes five years to recover? What if inflation stays at 5% for a decade? What if your partner can't work for medical reasons? What if your primary business faces regulatory shutdown? These aren't predictions. They are hypothetical audits. Each one asks: What breaks? What bends? What remains?

Importantly, don't confuse visibility with safety. People often feel secure because their accounts are up, or their lifestyle is unchanged. But stress-testing forces an uncomfortable discipline: examining the full financial architecture without being seduced by the superficial calm. The absence of visible threat does not mean the presence of underlying strength.

One of the best examples of proactive stress-testing comes from institutional investors. Endowments like Yale or MIT are required to plan for multi-year downturns, funding shocks, donor volatility, and liquidity freezes. Their investment committees don't merely debate performance—they analyse withdrawal rates, liability coverage, and operational runway. *This mindset is scalable.* A household can apply the same thinking: What are my minimum monthly obligations? What's my uncorrelated cash flow? If capital markets seize, how long can I fund this life without liquidating compromised assets?

A well-constructed stress-test culminates in a single question: *What would I regret not having done, if I knew this crisis was coming?* The answers often fall into patterns: I should have diversified income. I should have simplified my balance sheet. I should have made liquidity sacred. I should have communicated estate plans with my family. I should have reduced my lifestyle drag. I should have adjusted my ego to match my exposure.

These are not just financial acts. They are intellectual habits. They require humility, creativity, and a willingness to be briefly uncomfortable in exchange for enduring calm. Because what you discover in a stress-test isn't just what's missing from your setup—it's what kind of person you are when your setup gets tested.

And that may be the most important insight of all: *A resilient financial life isn't just a matter of what you hold—it's a reflection of how you think under pressure.* The goal isn't perfection. It's not even certainty. It's configuration: arranging your life so that when disruption comes—and it will—you bend without breaking, absorb without panicking, and continue forward without surrendering your agency.

Stress-testing is not for the paranoid. It is for the prepared. And in a world where fragility often hides behind polish, *the most underrated form of wealth is the ability to withstand what others can't even see coming.*

What You Can Copy (Without Millions)

One of the most dangerous assumptions in personal finance is that strategy scales with wealth. That the real playbook begins only once you cross some arbitrary threshold—£10 million in net worth, or a family office, or the right kind of trust fund. But this logic ignores a critical truth: *the architecture of enduring wealth is behavioural long before it is numerical.* High-net-worth individuals aren't just operating with more zeros; they're often operating with better models—models that can, in fact, be adopted at any level. The real barrier isn't capital—it's mindset, structure, and discipline.

To understand what can be copied without millions, begin not with tactics, but with orientation. Wealth preservation strategies are rarely reactive. They are engineered *before* success, not after. The rich who stay rich do not ask, "How much can I spend this year?" They ask, "What structure allows me to control volatility, obligation, and opportunity across decades?" *You do not need millions to ask that question well.*

Take legal infrastructure. Most people assume asset protection is a domain for billionaires with offshore entities and battery packs of lawyers. But the foundational principles are portable. Creating legal separation between personal and business assets, for example, is not expensive—it's about foresight. An entrepreneur earning £80,000 annually from a freelance consultancy should not wait until their earnings double before incorporating. *A limited company isn't just a tax vehicle—it's a firewall, a credibility signal, and a liability buffer.* Creating silos around streams of income, roles, and obligations is a habit of the financially secure, not merely the wealthy.

The same logic applies to estate thinking. You don't need a mansion or a multi-generational trust to write a will, assign powers of attorney, or organise beneficiaries across accounts. Most people procrastinate these moves under the illusion they're premature. But real wealth thinkers operate with the view that *clarity prevents conflict.* A basic living trust, even at modest net worth, offers control, reduces probate complexity, and signals maturity to your future self. It also trains the mind to think structurally—*not just emotionally—about mortality and transition.*

Then there's the realm of documentation. Family offices obsess over documentation—not because they like bureaucracy, but because they understand the cost of ambiguity. Cash flow plans, investment policies, tax projections, philanthropic aims—these are not just reference materials; they are cognitive anchors. Most people live without a written financial philosophy. They improvise. But the simple act of documenting your own rules—your thresholds for leverage, your triggers for selling, your guidelines for gifting—creates insulation. *Codifying your financial posture is a discipline that protects you from your own future inconsistency.*

But behaviours matter even more than frameworks. Among the rich, the most replicable habits are often the least flashy. Consider their relationship with information. While retail investors chase tips, many wealthy families operate with a rule: *act only on information that cannot be priced in.* They cultivate informational patience. They read transcripts, not headlines. They study footnotes, not Twitter threads. This isn't about IQ—it's about filtering inputs. Anyone, at any wealth level, can upgrade their sources and slow their reaction time. The result is not just better decisions, but *fewer decisions required*—an underrated lever of compounding sanity.

Another behaviour to copy is the strategic use of slowness. Wealthy individuals often move slower than they need to. They defer gratification not out of moral virtue, but because they understand sequence matters. They don't sprint into the first property they can afford—they wait for asymmetry. They don't dump excess capital into the market during euphoria—they keep dry powder. This is not procrastination. It is *optionality-preserving restraint.* You don't need millions to do this. You need the discipline to reject false urgency—a skill that pays higher returns than most investments.

An additional transferable habit is *asking "what breaks me?" before asking "what grows me?"* The rich build around downside exposure first. They rehearse ruin. You can do the same, even with modest assets. Ask: what's the single point of failure in your current financial life? What assumption, if false, would cascade into crisis? Is your income tied to one client? Is your rent or mortgage consuming more than 35% of take-home pay? Are your insurance coverages current, adequate, and uncorrelated to your employment? You don't need a financial adviser to answer these questions honestly. You need to *practice seeing yourself as a fragile system worth defending.*

Culturally, there is also much to copy. Enduring wealth is quiet wealth. It optimises for continuity, not applause. The deeply wealthy often drive unremarkable cars, wear understated clothing, and decline to broadcast their preferences. This is not always a strategy—it's a side effect of insulation from external validation. Yet it is copyable. Dressing neutrally, declining lifestyle inflation, and removing performative consumption from your default settings are acts of agency, not deprivation. They free capital for patience and prevent social signalling from cannibalising autonomy. *Understating your means is one of the highest-yielding forms of financial self-respect.*

Another underappreciated model is how the wealthy relate to advice. They outsource technically, but not blindly. They employ tax advisers, not because they're lazy, but because they respect leverage. But they also remain their own Chief Philosophy Officer. They *know how to ask better questions of their experts.* You don't need to hire a full advisory suite to start behaving this way. Begin by preparing more rigorously for meetings with your accountant or solicitor. Send agendas. Request specific modelling. Ask, "What assumptions are you making in this strategy?" or "What are the edge cases where this fails?" These are questions that *increase your competence and reduce reliance without control.*

It is also worth noting that the wealth-minded separate consumption from identity. Most people do not. They buy things to say things. But the durable rich treat purchases as tools, not metaphors. You can start this mindset now. Replace "Can I afford it?" with "What does this say about how I see myself?" and "Will this add stress, friction, or freedom?" The internal audit is portable. The wealthy simply do it with higher stakes.

Let's not ignore information management. One of the most copyable advantages of the rich is how they document and track. Many operate with dashboards—net worth statements, cash flow heatmaps, liquidity ladders—not because they need the data to live, but because they *treat their household like a business.* Anyone can do this. A Google Sheet and discipline can replicate 90% of a high-fee financial software tool. What matters is the habit of tracking, not the complexity of the tool. *Clarity compounds. So does confusion. Your spreadsheets are mirrors.*

We should also examine time. The wealthy use time differently not because they own yachts, but because they *treat calendar control as the highest ROI decision.* They schedule strategy days. They conduct financial retrospectives. They set "no meeting" zones not just for rest, but for synthesis. You can copy this without privilege. Block a half-day each month to review your finances. Use the time not just to update balances, but to reassess the logic behind your choices. Ask: Is this still true? What has changed? What feels fragile? What am I tolerating that I shouldn't be?

Finally, the most powerful transferable model is *the habit of thinking in decades, but acting in seasons.* The wealthy do not let short-term noise disrupt long-term compounding—but they also stay nimble enough to adjust. You can replicate this by setting 10-year aims, but revisiting execution every 90 days. Long horizons clarify strategy. Short feedback loops improve tactics. It's not the planning that makes the difference—it's the cadence.

So, what can you copy without millions? Almost everything that matters. You can build redundancy. You can reduce complexity. You can separate your identity from your income. You can draft your principles. You can conduct retrospectives. You can operate with deliberate slowness. You can value insulation over applause. And you can start today—not when you "have enough," but precisely *so that you can keep whatever you do manage to build.* Because the most sustainable form of wealth is behavioural infrastructure. And that scales at any income level.

Thinking in Decades, Acting in Seasons

The most enduringly wealthy individuals do not think in years. They think in decades. But they do not *act* in decades—they act in seasons. That distinction is not semantic. It is strategic. The capacity to hold long-range clarity while operating with short-range flexibility is one of the most potent, transferable mental models in all of personal finance and strategic planning. Most people, by contrast, live in one of two traps: they either obsess over the immediate and neglect the structural, or they fixate on grand futures while ignoring present realities. *True insulation lies in doing neither.*

Thinking in decades forces you to escape the tyranny of noise. It elevates the horizon beyond market cycles, employment changes, and daily volatility. It shifts the centre of gravity from consumption to durability. Ask someone who has preserved wealth over generations about their decision framework, and you'll notice something curious: *their timelines don't bend around crises—they absorb them.* Their decisions are built to survive not just the next event, but a sequence of them. That's because they model their lives the way engineers model bridges—not for average days, but for storms.

Take investment strategy. While retail investors react to headlines and central bank whispers, long-term thinkers anchor around regime shifts. They ask: *what assumptions do I need to hold true over the next 10, 20, or 30 years to be solvent, independent, and antifragile?* They do not attempt to time entries or exits. They reduce the role of timing altogether. When acting in seasons, their posture may shift tactically—rebalance, harvest losses, delay spending—but their core allocation philosophy remains unmoved. They know that consistency in decade-thinking breeds outcomes no annual sprint can match.

The same applies to career capital. Most professionals are caught in seasonal noise—performance reviews, project cycles, promotion games. Those with decade-level orientation view their careers as compound portfolios of skill, access, reputation, and optionality. They don't chase every trend. They hedge against obsolescence through *stacked competencies*. They invest in asymmetric learning—skills that open multiple future paths, not just immediate output. Acting in seasons, they may accept roles for positioning rather than salary, or intentionally downshift to recalibrate. *Every season has a purpose, but not every season should determine the plan.*

Nowhere is this model more relevant than in financial resilience. Wealthy families who endure across generations apply decade-thinking to liquidity and leverage. They ask: if our inflows disappeared for five years, what stays intact? They don't build systems that need every variable to work—they assume some will fail. But their actions within seasons are dynamic. They don't passively wait for storms to pass; they trim sails, reroute, conserve. That duality—the fixed compass, flexible rudder—is precisely what allows endurance. You can emulate this. Build your savings and risk structures around *long-range failure-resistance*, and your behaviour around *short-range prudence*.

This isn't abstract. Consider your housing decisions. Most people buy or rent at the edge of their current income. They optimise for the season. But decade thinkers ask: *what is the true cost of this commitment across a full cycle of job shifts, family changes, health events, and economic turns?* They might choose a smaller property not because they cannot afford more, but because they are modelling stability, not peak performance. Acting in seasons, they may delay upgrades or postpone renovations to maintain liquidity. They don't fear looking conservative—they prioritise looking solvent. That's insulation in practice.

There's also a psychological power in this model. Long-term thinkers tend to experience less emotional volatility. Not because they are detached, but because they have a framework that contextualises setbacks. They view downturns as *events within an arc*, not defining endpoints. Acting in seasons, they adapt—they may cut spending, pause investments, or shift energy to protection mode—but they do so without panic. Their sense of direction remains intact. That calm is not a by-product of wealth; it is a result of *frame control.* You can build that frame. Write your 10-year statement of intent. Then revisit it quarterly, not daily. Anchor, then adjust.

One reason this model works is that time itself is not linear in impact. Most people radically overestimate what they can do in a month and underestimate what's possible in a decade. But if you align the two—*set decade-level aims and season-level actions*—you unlock compounding that looks like magic to outsiders. This is why so many enduringly wealthy individuals appear uncannily consistent. They aren't gifted with foresight; they're disciplined in horizon control. They treat time not just as a calendar but as a multiplier. Each season becomes a deliberate deposit toward a long-range future.

This model also reveals the limits of short-term optimisation. Chasing marginal gains in a single season—whether through aggressive investments, career overextension, or consumption leverage—often backfires when external conditions shift. By contrast, a decade-level orientation creates strategic slack. It allows for rest, reallocation, even failure, without systemic collapse. Acting in seasons, then, isn't about urgency—it's about tact. It's about knowing which quarter matters and which doesn't, and adjusting your pace accordingly. You can afford to be wrong in a season if you are directionally right across the decade.

We must also account for emotional energy. Long-term success isn't just financial—it's mental and relational. Decade thinkers invest in friendships, health, and integrity not because they pay off immediately, but because they *compound invisibly.* They schedule sabbaticals before burnout. They build rituals to reconnect with principles. Season by season, they act in alignment with the person they want to be in ten years. And that congruence—between action and aim—is what builds trust, both internally and externally. It is no coincidence that trust-rich individuals are often wealth-resilient too.

Even philanthropy and legacy planning benefit from this mindset. Thinking in decades shifts giving from reaction to vision. Rather than responding to requests, the wealthy design impact portfolios—causes, communities, and institutions they want to shape over time. Acting in seasons, they experiment, pilot, adjust. They learn from results and revise the strategy. This creates a more authentic and effective giving model, one rooted not in guilt or optics, but in intentional stewardship. Anyone can copy this. Define a giving goal for 10 years, then build a seasonal cadence to move towards it with dignity and data.

Critically, this model also builds immunity to cultural whiplash. In a world that fetishises immediacy—viral success, quarterly returns, hot takes—the ability to operate on a different clock is an advantage. It grants independence of mind. You stop measuring yourself against metrics that reset every week. You develop what some call "temporal sovereignty"—the capacity to let time work for you, rather than constantly reacting to it. The wealthy who stay wealthy are almost always temporal sovereigns. They do not outsource their tempo.

So how does one begin? Start with clarity. Write your personal decade themes—health, relationships, wealth, knowledge, service. Under each, define what good looks like in ten years. Then define this season—90 days. What can be built, tested, refined? Then return to the map next season. Adjust, reallocate, but don't change the mountain unless new data demands it. This is not rigidity. This is *structured adaptability.* And it builds financial, emotional, and strategic insulation in ways that purely tactical planning never can.

Ultimately, thinking in decades but acting in seasons is not a productivity hack. It is a worldview. It allows you to live from a deeper place of clarity, to move through setbacks without collapse, to invest in what will matter long after this cycle, this crisis, or this quarter. It's how builders become stewards. It's how wealth becomes peace. And it's how, over time, what looks like caution becomes what others call genius.

The Wealth You Don't See

Ask someone on the street to picture a wealthy individual, and what they summon is rarely invisible. They see branded watches, pristine kitchens in glass-walled homes, luxury cars with custom stitching, first-class flights captured for social feed performance. What's almost never mentioned—but far more predictive of sustained affluence—is *what isn't seen.* Liquidity buffers. Trusts. Quiet ownership stakes. Durable health. Legal insulation. Intergenerational stability. Self-governance. The true architecture of wealth is concealed by design, not lack of means. *It's not that the enduringly wealthy avoid visibility by accident—it's that visible wealth often correlates with fragility, not insulation.*

In fact, visible wealth is frequently confused with financial security. But the former is a narrative; the latter is a structure. Consider the data: a household earning £200,000 annually in London, financing a £1.5 million home, leasing premium cars, sending children to private schools, and maintaining the appearances of affluence, may be asset-poor and exposure-rich. That same household could be one missed bonus or interest rate shock away from unraveling. Contrast this with a quieter family whose net worth is spread across diversified trusts, limited partnerships, cash-flowing businesses, and low-cost personal living. *The latter doesn't signal status but owns it outright.*

There is an uncomfortable truth embedded here: wealth that is truly durable often appears modest. It doesn't need applause. This principle is woven deeply into how generationally wealthy families operate. They define wealth as *options under pressure*, not purchases under calm. They don't need to prove anything externally, because their compounding operates internally. They can say no. They can pause. They can redirect. And critically, they can disappear from public gaze without losing momentum. That is the wealth most people never see.

The most sophisticated wealth managers often say their job is not to maximise returns—it's to maximise control. Control over time, over obligations, over jurisdictions, over succession. But control is invisible until it's tested. It looks like someone taking six months off to care for a loved one without changing lifestyle. It looks like a portfolio with modest returns that survives ten-year drawdowns intact. It looks like a middle-aged woman who owns equity in five quietly profitable companies but drives a ten-year-old car because she dislikes waste. *What you see says very little about what endures.*

This dissonance between perceived and actual wealth is amplified by digital culture. Social media accelerates the visibility game: influencers pose with borrowed watches, entrepreneurs celebrate fundraising rounds as if they're exits, and self-proclaimed moguls flaunt lifestyle perks that are often debt-financed. Meanwhile, the genuinely wealthy are notably absent. They hire reputation managers, not brand consultants. They pay for information security before they upgrade wardrobes. They structure their affairs to be legible to accountants, not to audiences. And their children are often taught, early and deliberately, to distinguish between liquidity and lifestyle.

Take the example of an ultra-high-net-worth family in Switzerland. Their primary residence is modest—a chalet that's been in the family for 60 years. The parents run a holding company that owns quiet stakes in logistics, infrastructure, and water rights across multiple geographies. No names on buildings. No family office Instagram accounts. Yet the structures in place are world-class: Swiss foundations for philanthropy, layered trusts across favourable jurisdictions, family governance protocols that rival mid-sized corporations. Their children attend ordinary public schools until secondary level. They understand that *the less the world sees, the more strategic room they have to manoeuvre.*

This isn't simply cultural—it's strategic. Visibility invites scrutiny, competition, litigation, and envy. But invisible wealth moves through systems differently. It flows, it compounds, and it escapes detection. The best private equity deals never reach the public. The most resilient portfolios aren't sexy—they're sleepable. The most effective family legacies are maintained not through estates, but through values, behaviours, and internal institutions. And yet none of these are broadcast. *The more performative your wealth, the less time you have to deepen it.*

Philosophically, this calls for a reframing: wealth is not a number, but a system. And the most robust systems are ones where internal coherence is prioritised over external signalling. That means alignment between income sources and expenditures, legal structures and citizenship status, family culture and capital deployment. It also means actively avoiding configurations that require constant performance to stay intact. Flashy lifestyles become prisons when the conditions to sustain them are narrow. Quiet wealth, by contrast, grows in silence because it's decoupled from approval.

This also explains the behavioural norms of enduringly wealthy families. They develop habits that intentionally avoid wealth cues. Understated clothing. Unbranded vehicles. Neutral speech. Low exposure to media. Conversations are not about what was bought, but about what was built, stewarded, protected. They understand that discretion is not timidity—it is defence. Visibility increases surface area. It draws in predators, noise, and complexity. True insulation begins where public performance ends.

What does this mean for someone building wealth without generational assets behind them? First, it means defining success by *freedom of choice*, not visibility of lifestyle. Can you miss six months of income and remain solvent? Can you relocate without asking permission? Can you support dependents without sacrificing long-term solvency? These are the questions that quiet wealth answers yes to. Second, it means focusing on building assets and systems that don't depend on constant maintenance: businesses with operating teams, portfolios with low drag, income streams not tied to personal charisma.

It also means embracing invisibility as a superpower. Let others chase likes. Let them optimise for optical success. Your goal is to create a private empire of control, not a public illusion of prestige. That means boring financial planning, aggressive debt reduction, strategic tax literacy, and privacy-by-design. These aren't glamorous.

But they are repeatable. And they scale. *There is a dignity in wealth that doesn't seek applause—it simply works.*

Interestingly, many of the wealthiest people in the world are surrounded by less-visible peers who hold enormous influence without ever making a list. The policy donors behind institutions. The controlling shareholders behind conglomerates. The multigenerational landholders with rights to natural resources. They sit behind structures that do the speaking for them. Their names may be absent, but their fingerprints are everywhere—on decisions, on outcomes, on capital flows. And yet to the average observer, they blend in. That blending is not accidental. It is cultivated.

There's also an emotional aspect to invisible wealth that's often overlooked. It breeds *calm*. Not because it removes hardship, but because it removes performance pressure. You no longer need to posture. You no longer need to compete on surface metrics. You can detach your identity from volatility. And in doing so, you recover time, energy, presence. Many quiet wealthy individuals report feeling less anxious, less reactive, and more present in their relationships. They are no longer actors in someone else's narrative. They are authors of their own.

For readers navigating financial ambition, the invitation is not to reject wealth, but to reframe it. Let your wealth be something that buys you time, privacy, access, leverage, and trust. Let it be something that deepens your character, not distorts your identity. Let it insulate, not inflate. When you do that, you begin to experience the real power of money—not in what it shows others, but in what it frees you to do *without needing their permission.*

The wealth you don't see is the wealth you can rely on. It's the wealth that works when you're not watching it. It's the wealth that doesn't need defending because it hasn't been broadcast. It's the trust fund structured for five generations. The unleveraged asset producing modest but stable cash flow. The investor who has nothing flashy but owns equity in quiet monopolies. The family whose spending is half of what it could be, not because of fear, but because they have enough—and know it.

Visibility is not proof. Validation is not insulation. Wealth is what holds its shape when the spotlight moves. And more often than not, *the wealth that stays is the wealth that hides.*

Chapter 11
Endurance Over Expansion

The allure of permanence in wealth is one of modern society's most beguiling illusions. Yet history delivers a clear verdict: fortunes built on velocity rarely endure. They surge into view with the thrill of disruption, scale with evangelical zeal, and then often dissipate quietly under the weight of unsustainable momentum. Expansion shouts; endurance whispers. In the realm of lasting affluence, triumph belongs not to the accelerators, but to those who master the art of coasting without stalling. The question at the heart of this reflection is subtle, yet profound: might the ultimate luxury be less about spectacle, and more about staying power?

For most, progress is measured by movement—revenue, reach, recognition. But the long arc of preservation does not reward speed. It rewards resilience. Success is not what one can achieve in a bull market; it is what one can survive when conditions reverse. Endurance is not ambition's enemy. It is its sober companion—one that understands how to pace itself, protect compounding, and tolerate obscurity without anxiety. Those who preserve wealth across generations do not chase visibility; they design redundancy at every layer: cash, cognition, geography, identity.

This is not philosophical abstraction. The evidence is unmistakable. Enduring fortunes adhere to principles that diverge sharply from growth-obsessed corporate cultures and consumerist models. They embrace deliberate under-optimisation: not maxing every return, not stretching every dollar, not filling every calendar slot. In doing so, they preserve optionality. Short-term efficiency is traded for long-term adaptability, because fragile optimisation is more dangerous than robust imperfection.

These families, entities, and individuals do not track success by quarterly deltas. Their scorecards are orthogonal to public benchmarks. How many income streams survive market turbulence? How many decisions require no external permissions? How many obligations can be delayed without consequence? How many crises could be weathered without behavioural compromise? These are not hypothetical queries—they are actively measured, revisited, and engineered for by quietly enduring dynasties.

Here lies a paradox of modern wealth narratives: the obsession with accumulation often undermines the very systems that sustain it. Consider the tech founder who expands too fast, overcommits capital, and overexposes themselves. Or the executive who confuses prestige for protection. Or the inheritor seeking validation through exposure rather than stewardship. In each instance, the failure is conceptual as much as tactical—they are playing for expansion in a game that ultimately punishes visibility.

To endure, one must redefine success: not as accumulation of assets, but as control over variables; not as linear growth, but as regenerative equilibrium; not as public attention, but as structural autonomy. The enduringly wealthy ask, "How little can I lose?" rather than "How much can I earn?" They hedge against the irreversible, cultivate decision latitude under constraint, and prioritise resilience over performance metrics.

This posture is forged through experience. Multi-generational family offices carry scars from events that defied prediction—regime changes, currency collapses, asset seizures, war, political upheaval, private betrayals. Exposure to structural rupture teaches the mind to favour redundancy over leverage, discretion over display. They recognise that the next systemic shock is rarely the one anticipated.

Endurance is forward-facing. It is not nostalgic. It adapts, scenario-plans, and remains vigilant. Wealth in motion is wealth at risk; the question becomes: what will the next crisis reward? Patterns emerge—liquidity, mobility, unencumbered ownership, a bias toward simplicity, and above all, the capacity to respond from structure, not impulse.

Consider the contrast during the COVID-19 crisis. High-profile businesses, burdened with overhead and scrutiny, scrambled to react. Meanwhile, private families with layered trusts, hard assets, low leverage, and decentralised income watched and waited. They had prepared their oxygen tanks years in advance. Their portfolios were not heroic—they were sleepable. Stress was strategic, not existential.

Endurance also shapes legacy—not merely as asset inheritance, but as a transmission of systems thinking. The wealthy leave behind frameworks for navigating uncertainty: decision-making protocols, governance norms, identities decoupled from net worth. This is legacy as epistemology, not capital—teaching the next generation to distinguish signal from noise, to manage decline, and, crucially, to pause. To walk away from a deal, to hold cash, to do nothing when inaction is the wisest move. Emotional discipline compounds, quietly but powerfully.

Early in wealth-building, such virtues are often undervalued. Yet enduring capital is not born from bravado. It emerges from patience, structure, clarity, and restraint. Resilient wealth has no slogans. It has protocols, buffers, and mental habits that resist the cultural pull toward more, faster, louder. It is, at its essence, duration without distortion.

Ultimately, staying rich is not about acceleration—it is about becoming unshakeable. Strength is measured not by how quickly one grows, but by how thoroughly one can endure what shatters others. Wealth is not merely what we build—it is what we withstand, and what remains once the imperative to prove it has passed.

Why Staying Rich Is a Slower, Quieter Game

The most enduring financial empires are often the least conspicuous. Their owners don't attend launch parties or boast earnings on social media. They don't chase yield in every market or optimise every calendar quarter. Instead, they practice something deceptively rare in the modern economy: they *wait.* While others measure success by speed, status, or scale, those who remain wealthy over generations calibrate their lives around *duration.* They're not interested in being seen winning—only in not losing. *True wealth is not earned once—it is outlasted repeatedly.*

The idea that wealth can be "achieved" is itself misleading. Wealth is not a static destination. It is a moving system that must be stabilised, stewarded, and immunised against entropy. The public tends to fixate on the "getting"—how a fortune was made—but far fewer interrogate the equally complex problem of the *keeping*. And that is precisely where speed becomes a liability. Accelerated success may win headlines, but it rarely builds endurance. Sustained wealth—*quiet, stress-resistant, intergenerational capital*—requires the opposite: deliberate pacing, strategic patience, and the restraint to *not optimise every variable.*

This becomes clearer when one contrasts two competing archetypes: the entrepreneur who burns through three hyper-growth ventures in a decade, and the family business that grows revenues at 2% per year, pays no dividends, avoids debt, and survives three recessions. The former lives in acceleration mode—rewarded by media, venture capital, and narrative. The latter endures in obscurity—ignored by magazines but cherished by heirs. *Which model is more resilient when the system resets?* Acceleration may dazzle, but endurance dominates when time is given a chance to vote.

This reframing of wealth as *endurance* invites a deeper examination of what actually causes collapse. Historically, the decline of great fortunes rarely stems from lack of innovation or misjudged investment alone. More often, it is *exposure without insulation*—legal, emotional, and reputational. A liquidity squeeze at the wrong time. An overleveraged position justified by short-term returns. A lifestyle calibrated for boom cycles, unable to scale down with grace. These aren't failures of intelligence—they're failures of pacing. Of forgetting that *staying rich is less about new wins, and more about not creating new vulnerabilities.*

When speed becomes a cultural imperative, fragility often follows. Consider the proliferation of debt-fuelled expansion across sectors—from real estate empires to private equity to consumer startups. The logic is simple: move faster, borrow more, scale quickly. But this logic assumes a predictable backdrop. Once conditions turn volatile, speed has no margin for error. The families and individuals who survive financial winters are often those who prepared for them—not because they predicted the specific cause, but because they never assumed predictability in the first place.

Herein lies the philosophical core of slow wealth: *risk is not an event, it is a constant.* Those who endure act accordingly. They do not try to game the system for maximum exposure. Instead, they design their financial lives around margin—buffers in liquidity, lifestyle, geography, and emotional bandwidth. Their core asset is *optionality*, not optimisation. They don't overfit to market cycles. They don't run lean at all costs. They don't need every investment to work. They only need a few to survive.

This slower rhythm manifests in practical behaviours. Wealth that lasts is rarely flamboyant. It's cautious with visibility, because visibility invites claims—from media, tax authorities, opportunists, or political antagonists. It's slow to scale lifestyle, even when net worth increases, because cost structures are hard to reverse. It's suspicious of short-term outperformance, preferring instead the compound returns of safe, boring, repeatable systems. It places *governance before growth*, insisting that internal controls, clarity of ownership, and succession plans exist long before they are needed.

And perhaps most strikingly, it sees no urgency to be understood. The enduringly wealthy are not interested in explaining their approach to outsiders. They don't argue on the internet. They don't promote themselves as thought leaders. They cultivate silence—not because they have something to hide, but because they *value insulation more than approval.* Their game is not to convince, but to continue. Not to win today, but to remain free tomorrow.

This tension—between speed and stability, between visibility and longevity—runs throughout the history of private capital. In the post-war period, many European industrial families quietly moved assets across borders, established generational trusts, and invested in long-dated infrastructure projects that paid off decades later. Meanwhile, in faster economies like the United States, fortunes rose and fell with public market volatility, founder personalities, or regulatory tides. Speed, for all its glamour, rarely offers shelter.

There are instructive lessons here for anyone building or managing wealth at any scale. The same principles that insulate the billion-dollar family office also apply to a professional managing a six-figure portfolio. The core idea is this: *structure outlives strategy.* Anyone can get lucky for a few years. But only those with strong financial and emotional structures survive the full arc of volatility. That means legal entities that shield assets from direct exposure. That means cashflow streams that don't depend on single counterparties. That means personal routines that prioritise clarity over urgency. These are not exotic tools—they're available to anyone willing to trade adrenaline for architecture.

The myth of rapid wealth also suffers from psychological fragility. A person who gets rich quickly often builds their identity around that velocity. But once market conditions change—or if a public failure occurs—that identity becomes brittle. Contrast that with someone who sees wealth as a custodial responsibility, not a performative symbol. They may feel no pressure to upgrade their car, their postcode, or their wardrobe—even after a liquidity event. Their relationship to money is not defined by speed of acquisition, but by *continuity of agency.*

Continuity, in this context, is everything. Not just the continuity of capital, but of *calm decision-making, unrushed timelines, unpanicked behaviour.* Speed creates demands on cognition. It erodes patience, narrows perspective, and invites error. That's why those who endure often build decision calendars that deliberately slow them down. They don't check markets daily. They rarely pivot based on noise. They know that many great financial decisions feel boring at the time. And they are fine with that. Because *boring compounds.*

The obsession with acceleration also distorts definitions of success. When status is defined by external validation—likes, awards, appearances—there's always pressure to stay in motion. But when success is redefined as *optionality, privacy, resilience*, and *low dependence*, a slower game becomes not only acceptable, but optimal. This isn't about being risk-averse. It's about being *asymmetrically positioned*: willing to take risks from a place of strength, not desperation.

Staying rich, then, is not about brilliance. It's about posture. Not the performative posture of status signalling, but the structural posture of someone who doesn't need to chase. Who can afford to decline invitations. Who chooses margin over maximisation. And who understands that the best-performing asset over time is *control over one's own pace.*

In the final assessment, staying rich requires discipline that feels invisible from the outside. It's not just about investments, but about rhythm—what you say no to, how slowly you scale, which battles you avoid. The slower game is not less ambitious. It is simply more *durable.* It is played not for the approval of others, but for the quiet satisfaction of freedom, continuity, and peace. Those who learn this lesson early may never be the loudest in the room. But they will likely be the last ones still standing.

A New Scorecard

If your definition of financial success still rests on income, assets, or net worth, you're playing by an outdated metric system—one designed for visibility, not resilience. The problem is not that these markers are irrelevant; it's that they are dangerously incomplete. In an increasingly complex, high-volatility world, conventional financial metrics reveal only the surface conditions of wealth, not its structural integrity. What matters more than the size of your balance sheet is the *shape* of your exposure. In truth, the most enduring wealth is rarely the most impressive on paper—it is the hardest to disrupt, the least dependent on external validation, and the most insulated from systemic shocks. *Power that doesn't announce itself is often the most potent kind.*

We need a new scorecard. One that prizes *optionality over optimisation*, *quiet power over public dominance*, and *exposure control over asset accumulation.* The old model—maximise income, accumulate visible assets, signal success—is not only fragile; it's increasingly maladaptive. It produces high burn rates, shallow buffers, and a relentless pressure to perform. The new model is slower, less visible, but exponentially more robust. It asks not "How much do you own?" but "How much could you afford to lose without your life being disrupted?" and more importantly, "Who or what controls the terms of your existence?"

Consider this: Two individuals both earn £400,000 a year. One lives in a high-cost urban centre, with three properties on interest-only mortgages, a child in private school, and a lifestyle contingent on a bonus cycle. The other lives modestly, with low fixed costs, holds liquid reserves, and owns assets in uncorrelated jurisdictions. One is rich by traditional scorecards. The other is wealthy by the metrics that actually matter in a downturn. *Real financial strength is not what you show. It's what you can survive.*

The first and perhaps most overlooked new metric is *optionality*. Optionality is the freedom to make choices without coercion. It is the opposite of financial entrapment. When you possess optionality, you can say no—to clients, to locations, to employment, to exposure—because your baseline is stable. Optionality is built through cash reserves, mobile income streams, low fixed liabilities, and jurisdictions that allow for exit. In contrast, someone earning millions a year with no buffer, no privacy, and no exit strategy is effectively *trapped by their own success.*

Quiet power is another under-recognised dimension. It has nothing to do with influence over others and everything to do with control over one's circumstances. Quiet power means you are hard to manipulate. Your lifestyle cannot be easily cancelled, your business model does not rely on staying culturally relevant, and your family's legal setup cannot be unwound by a single court ruling. You are not necessarily anonymous, but your centre of gravity is hard to dislodge. You hold multiple passports, diversified structures, and employ advisors whose job is to keep you uninteresting to the public eye. Quiet power is built in silence, maintained through discretion, and exercised through well-insulated leverage. It is a game of restraint, not dominance.

Then there is exposure control—the art of not being overleveraged to any one outcome, institution, narrative, or person. The new scorecard must account for *correlated risk*, not just isolated holdings. If all your assets depend on fiat currency, national policy, or a single economic zone, your wealth may be larger than most, but it is still brittle. Similarly, if your identity is tethered to a personal brand, your income to a sponsor, or your liquidity to market sentiment, then your autonomy is an illusion. Controlling exposure doesn't mean eliminating risk; it means *designing a system where risks don't compound into existential threats.*

This new scorecard also demands a reevaluation of what counts as productive capital. The wealthy used to be praised for their asset bases—property portfolios, equity stakes, luxury collections. But in an age where capital markets are increasingly interdependent and exposed to geopolitical swings, more is not always safer. *It's not the volume of assets but the velocity and volatility they carry* that should inform one's assessment. A modest holding in a well-governed, boring jurisdiction may offer more endurance than a trophy asset in a flashy but unstable economy.

The enduringly wealthy understand this. They use trusts not to hide wealth but to *decentralise control and limit liability*. They hold uncorrelated assets—not because they're trendy, but because they understand systemic cycles. They buy time, not toys. They spend on resilience infrastructure, not recognition optics. They optimise for *breathing room*, not maximum yield. Their real wealth is measured in the ability to move without consequence, to pause without panic, to pivot without peril.

This stands in sharp contrast to the high-income earners who mistake velocity for security. A surgeon making £500,000 a year in a single country with a rigid schedule and high burn rate is arguably less financially resilient than a writer earning £80,000 across geographies with no fixed overhead. *Income is not insulation.* Control over time, jurisdictional flexibility, and the absence of urgent dependencies are far more predictive of long-term wealth preservation than the number on a payslip.

One might ask: how does one begin to adopt this new scorecard in practical terms? The answer lies less in what you own and more in how you *structure* what you own. Do your legal entities protect your assets from liability or simply hold them? Is your income stream dependent on a single platform, employer, or sector? Are your lifestyle costs fixed or discretionary? Are your assets visible to the wrong audiences—governments, ex-spouses, or opportunistic creditors? These are not paranoid questions—they are pragmatic ones. *The more publicly visible your wealth, the more privately vulnerable you become.*

This paradigm shift also requires emotional recalibration. The old scorecard rewarded urgency, growth, and showmanship. The new one rewards patience, redundancy, and restraint. It forces you to ask harder questions: How many days could I go without income before I make a compromised decision? What percentage of my net worth can be accessed without bureaucratic delay? If I were falsely accused in a high-profile setting, how well could my financial structures withstand reputational damage? These are uncomfortable reflections. But they're also where *real power begins.*

It's important, too, to understand that this reframing is not about asceticism or fear. It is about *sovereignty.* A sovereign financial life is not one without ambition—it is one where ambition is not tethered to fragility. You can still grow, scale, and enjoy. But you grow on your terms. You scale when conditions permit. You enjoy from a place of internal safety, not social expectation.

Ultimately, the new scorecard is an invitation to stop playing games you cannot win. To stop competing on visibility. To stop measuring success by metrics that are easy to fake and hard to sustain. Instead, it calls for a shift in how you define your edge. Not louder. Not faster. *Just harder to compromise.*

In a world obsessed with metrics, we need better ones. Ones that reward *quiet insulation over noisy accumulation.* Ones that reflect not what you earn, but what you can walk away from. Ones that measure strength not in moments of triumph, but in times of stress. This is the real scoreboard of the enduringly wealthy. And it's not broadcasted anywhere. Because the most reliable metrics, like the most resilient fortunes, tend to operate best in silence.

What the Next Crisis Will Reward

History does not repeat itself, but it often reintroduces the same exam questions under new disguises. And when the next systemic crisis arrives—whether triggered by geopolitical disruption, technological displacement, resource instability, or the quiet unravelling of overleveraged systems—the scoreboard for who thrives and who fractures will not be determined by who appeared most successful in the years prior. It will be determined by structures, habits, and positioning—by decisions made long before urgency demanded them. The next crisis will not reward brilliance, scale, or charisma. It will reward *resilience without visibility*, *liquidity without dependence*, and *structure without spectacle.*

During the 2008 financial crisis, institutions that once seemed unshakeable collapsed in weeks. It was not the most leveraged, but the most *interconnected* players who suffered existential consequences. Lehman Brothers did not fail solely because of exposure to toxic assets, but because its collapse threatened to trigger systemic seizures across counterparties, governments, and clients. In contrast, firms that maintained conservative leverage ratios, decentralised risk across jurisdictions, and avoided visibility-based overconfidence weathered the storm—not because they were smarter, but because they were *structurally less exposed to contagion.* The same logic applies on a personal level. When disruption comes, it will not be your ambition or your assets that save you. It will be *how few points of failure you've left in your life and financial ecosystem.*

The next crisis will reward redundancy—specifically, those who have designed their lives and holdings to operate under multiple conditions, not just the optimal one. Most people and firms operate with efficiency as their north star. They optimise for the present, streamline costs, and bet heavily on a single favourable trajectory. But resilience and efficiency rarely coexist. Resilience demands *slack in the system*—unproductive cash, unused bandwidth, optionality that feels wasteful in normal conditions. In an efficiency-obsessed economy, slack looks like weakness. Until it becomes your lifeboat.

Those who will outperform in the next shock will not be the ones who guessed the cause correctly, but those who built structures flexible enough to *absorb surprise without capitulation.* This includes having multiple banking relationships across uncorrelated jurisdictions, access to offline or alternative liquidity mechanisms, asset protections that outlast market freezes, and legal entities not confined to a single flag. It includes a professional life not overindexed on a single brand, employer, or audience platform. And perhaps most importantly, it includes *a psyche trained not to panic at volatility*, but to interpret chaos as part of the design.

Much has been written about antifragility—systems that improve through stress rather than merely survive it. But the trait even rarer, and more rewarded, is *pre-stress calibration.* The wealthy who endure are not simply those who recover quickly; they are those who barely flinch because they've already performed a pre-mortem. They've gamed out scenarios—market freezes, lawsuits, cyber breaches, institutional insolvency—and quietly built layers of insulation against them. Their confidence isn't performative; it's architectural.

It is also jurisdictional. Many of the individuals best positioned to ride out future dislocations have *deliberately detached themselves from single-state dependency.* They understand that legal risk is geographic risk. Political narratives change. Capital controls emerge. Tax codes shift. The next crisis is likely to involve not just asset volatility, but *governance volatility.* The structures that endure will be those designed to *operate across multiple legal environments*, often with one eye on what is technically allowed and another on what is socially tolerated. Trusts, holding companies, and private agreements that were once dismissed as tools for the ultra-wealthy are increasingly becoming *essential infrastructure for autonomy.*

Equally, the next crisis will reward *informational asymmetry.* Not secrecy, but *disciplined informational exposure.* Those who have minimised their public digital footprint, maintained ambiguity about their liquidity, and refused to signal upward economic mobility too visibly will enjoy insulation—not just from opportunistic threats, but from political and legal pressures that often follow perceived success. In contrast, those who have mistaken visibility for safety will find themselves overexposed, under-defended, and out of allies. *When pressure rises, what you signal becomes what you must defend.*

This is not paranoia; it is pattern recognition. In each major dislocation, the friction is not distributed evenly. It flows toward perceived stability, toward liquidity pockets, toward those who failed to understand that being solvent and being *accessible* are not the same thing. The structures that succeed will be those that *obscure their own strength*—not to deceive, but to preserve. Wealth, when visible, becomes an invitation for negotiation, litigation, and appropriation. Wealth, when discretely structured and legally fortified, becomes irrelevant to the public imagination—and thus, *safer to preserve and transmit.*

The next crisis will also reward *psychological autonomy*. In times of systemic stress, narrative control fragments. Media institutions weaken. Authorities contradict each other. The people who remain grounded are those who have already developed *epistemic independence*—the ability to assess information without being swept by collective panic or tribal thinking. This is not an abstract skill; it translates directly into decisions about where to move capital, when to exit markets, which partners to trust, and when to sit still. *Panic is rarely about money. It is about narrative disintegration.* Those who have prepared for that internally will have an unquantifiable edge.

At the level of behaviour, endurance during crisis often comes down to *unsexy discipline*. Those who have maintained low fixed costs, cultivated high cash optionality, said no to leverage even when it was fashionable, and stayed outside attention-driven economies will find that their dull habits were their most important assets. They will not need to sell into panic, relocate under duress, or reinvent their strategy mid-collapse. The systems they have built were *never optimised for celebration. They were optimised for silence under pressure.*

This also includes relational capital. The next crisis will reward those who invested in *trust before they needed it.* Not performative networks or transactional alliances, but deep relationships forged through discretion, competence, and time. When institutions wobble and supply chains fracture, those who can call on trusted humans—not brands—will find themselves with access, liquidity, and opportunities that cannot be replicated last-minute. And again, the key is advance design: *you cannot fake reliability in a crisis. You either built it before or you go without it.*

None of this should be confused with survivalism or isolation. The aim is not to outlast the world, but to remain *a stable node when everything else is flickering*. Stability attracts trust, opportunity, and leverage. The individuals and entities who remain calm, credible, and operational while others are improvising in panic will emerge with disproportionate influence—not because they manipulated the crisis, but because *they designed their systems not to need perfect conditions.*

There is no predictive model precise enough to tell us what the next crisis will look like. But there are *patterns of fragility* that consistently precede collapse: overdependence on institutions, underestimation of tail risk, performative visibility, single-point exposure, and psychological brittleness. The inverse of these patterns is where the enduring build their edge—not through foresight, but through *preparation for structural ignorance*. They don't claim to know what's coming. They claim only to have *made peace with not knowing—and acted accordingly.*

When the rules break, the scoreboard resets. And in that reset, endurance becomes the new prestige. Quiet competence, once overlooked, becomes premium. Optionality, once mocked as indecision, becomes a currency. And the systems that once looked overly conservative begin to look like *the only rational response to uncertainty.*

The next crisis will reward the invisible choices—the ones made when no one was watching, when panic wasn't present, and when no applause was expected. Because those are the choices that cannot be retrofitted. They are earned only in advance.

The Legacy You Engineer

Legacy is commonly reduced to what is inherited—property, cash, reputations secured by surname, or foundations bearing a family crest. But what if legacy is not what is handed down, but what *replicates itself without your supervision*? What if the most durable form of inheritance is not capital, but cognition—not the sum total of what you owned, but the architecture of how you thought?

Every fortune eventually finds itself managed by someone else. What distinguishes lasting influence from fleeting wealth is the presence—or absence—of *inheritable mental frameworks*. True legacy is not trust-fund stewardship; it is intellectual scaffolding that endures beyond the founder. It is *cultural DNA deliberately encoded into others*, not just biologically, but mentally—through decision templates, heuristic structures, values under pressure, and the quiet transmission of models for navigating uncertainty.

The most enduring dynasties, family offices, and institutions do not pass on instructions. They pass on frameworks. The Rothschilds did not survive for two centuries because they memorised market trends; they handed down operating systems—ways of seeing asymmetry, managing risk, navigating discretion, and aligning cross-border interests. Similarly, the modern billionaire who quietly ensures their children *understand leverage before they understand lifestyle* is doing more to secure generational success than any inheritance tax strategy ever could.

Yet, this form of engineered legacy is strikingly rare. Many wealth transitions fail—not because the assets weren't sufficient, but because the mindset attached to them was never taught, absorbed, or even discussed. Most high-net-worth families spend years optimising for legal efficiency and tax sheltering, while allocating almost no time to the *transmission of epistemic integrity*: how to distinguish signal from noise, how to operate under ambiguity, how to assess people and institutions, how to build conviction without visibility. These are the tools that actually preserve wealth—and identity—over time. They cannot be outsourced, and they rarely emerge spontaneously in the next generation.

If wealth is to endure, its accompanying logic must be *explicitly encoded*. Otherwise, all that remains is surface inheritance—beneficiaries who have money, but not the lens through which the money was originally created and protected. This is where engineered legacy begins: *codifying the thinking before codifying the assets*. Consider the difference between teaching someone *what to buy* versus *how to evaluate any investment opportunity under changing conditions*. One is a transaction; the other is a transferable mental model. The latter survives you.

Engineered legacy also demands conscious modelling. Children and successors don't internalise advice nearly as effectively as they absorb patterns. The way you react to uncertainty, the people you choose to surround yourself with, how you behave under reputational threat, how you deal with failure—these are all educational scripts. If your decision-making process is opaque or emotionally reactive, your legacy will not be resilient; it will be performative. To engineer a lasting legacy, your conduct must *model the thinking you wish to replicate*, even when it's inconvenient or invisible to the outside world.

This is especially important because the environments your successors will inherit are not yours. They will operate under different rules, cultural norms, and technologies. What matters most is not preparing them for *your world*, but preparing them to *operate adaptively in any world.* That means emphasising enduring concepts over transient knowledge. Legal codes shift, asset classes evolve, regimes rise and fall. But *understanding game theory, power asymmetry, second-order consequences, and institutional fragility*—these frameworks travel well across time. They are your intellectual real estate.

Engineered legacy also manifests in *what you choose not to prioritise.* Many individuals unintentionally pass down insecurity by encoding fear-based scarcity narratives: don't trust outsiders, don't take risks, avoid visibility. Others pass down reputational obsessions—live up to the name, protect the brand, preserve appearances. These mental blueprints often cause more harm than good. A better model begins with questions like: *What assumptions do I operate from that have served me well? Which of these can be articulated clearly enough to guide others without my presence?* The answers to these questions form the basis of a portable intellectual inheritance.

None of this replaces formal estate planning—it complements it. Trusts, legal wrappers, asset structures—all of these are important. But without mental clarity embedded in the beneficiaries, they act as temporary armour at best. Long-term preservation requires that you *replicate capacity, not just protect capital.* This might include structured education—training successors to understand how their family's wealth was built and what fragilities it faces. It might involve scenario planning—walking through plausible future crises and encouraging independent decision-making under stress. It might simply mean building a shared language of thought—so that, when volatility arrives, your heirs aren't just asking, "What would they have done?" but rather, "How would they have thought about this?"

Crucially, engineered legacy doesn't require vast resources. Even those of modest means can pass on powerful thinking systems. A small business owner who teaches their children how to analyse contracts, interpret supplier incentives, or negotiate from strength has passed on more utility than someone who leaves behind a sprawling portfolio but no strategic sensibility. Similarly, a parent who models composure during financial turbulence, who refrains from performative wealth, who demonstrates curiosity and integrity in everyday decisions—this is legacy, *embedded in behaviour rather than bequeathed in documents.*

Legacy, when stripped of its performative layer, becomes *the cultivation of strategic self-sufficiency in others.* Not dependence, not obedience, not even gratitude. Just the capacity to operate with clarity under changing conditions. This is why the wealthiest families often invest heavily in education, exposure, and values development—not for optics, but because they understand that capital without comprehension is not inheritance, it is burden.

This reframing of legacy also has broader cultural implications. When society sees legacy primarily as intergenerational privilege, the assumption is that inequality is compounded through static capital. But if legacy were reconceived as *a set of skills, values, and decision frameworks actively taught*, it invites a different standard: one where the real privilege is epistemic, not material. And that kind of privilege can, in fact, be decentralised—through writing, mentorship, institution-building, and narrative transparency.

At its best, engineered legacy becomes *non-exclusive.* It transcends lineage and becomes part of cultural infrastructure. The thinking frameworks that once lived in private family offices, elite law firms, or bespoke investment circles can now be written, shared, and taught—without dilution. Books, private letters, enduring educational models—these are the tools of posthumous influence. This book, in many ways, is an attempt to democratise those very blueprints: not to mimic the rich, but to *translate how they think in a way that others can adapt, improve, and deploy.*

In the final accounting, the wealth that survives you will be measured not in zeros but in the number of people who continue to *think more clearly because you existed.* Not in what they remember, but in how they reason. Not in the size of your name, but in the durability of your thought. That is the legacy you engineer—not once at the end of your life, but every day you decide to act with foresight, integrity, and transferability in mind.

The ultimate test of influence is whether your presence remains *useful* after your departure. The quiet systems you leave behind—in people, processes, principles—become the real monument. Not statues, not memoirs. *Structures of thought that outlive the thinker.* That, and only that, is the legacy worth building.

About the Author

Julian C. Vale writes about the intersection of wealth, risk, and strategic behavior with an eye for what endures. Known for dissecting complex systems in clear, accessible language, Vale's work is shaped by years observing how individuals and institutions navigate volatility—not just to win, but to last. His approach is neither alarmist nor idealistic. He believes in clarity over hype, frameworks over fads, and resilience over endless growth. Julian's passion lies in equipping readers with mental models that sharpen perception and upgrade decision-making—especially in times of uncertainty.

www.ingramcontent.com/pod-product-compliance
Lightning Source LLC
Chambersburg PA
CBHW031346230926
51848CB00002B/403
* 9 7 8 9 3 7 1 7 7 0 0 6 4 *